EARTH
WATER
AND FIRE

EARTH
WATER
AND FIRE

THE PREHISTORIC POTTERY OF MESA VERDE

NORMAN T. OPPELT

Johnson Books: Boulder

Cover design by Bob Schram

Cover photograph: Mesa Verde White Ware and Corrugated Gray Ware pottery
vessels in Cliff House, Mesa Verde National Park. (*Courtesy MVNP*)

ISBN 1-55566-085-1
LCCCN 91-75686

Printed in the United States of America by
Johnson Publishing Company
1880 South 57th Court
Boulder, Colorado 80301

PRINTED WITH
SOY INK

CONTENTS

Dedication

This book is dedicated to Paul Ermigiotti of Crow Canyon Archaeological Center and Linda Martin, Mesa Verde National Park. Paul shares my intense interest in, and love for, the fascinating prehistoric pottery of the Southwest. Through our experimental firings and many discussions, he has shared his insights into how this pottery was made. Without his energy, encouragement, and artistic contributions, this book would not have been written.

Linda Martin has broader knowledge of Mesa Verde than any other current staff member. She has encouraged me in this research, and after carefully reading the first draft, she made many valuable suggestions. Linda, through her training and supervision of the seasonal rangers at Mesa Verde, has helped millions of visitors to have a better understanding of the ancient Anasazi and their world.

FOREWORD

Anasazi pottery is a durable legacy of a people who stayed for a while in the Four Corners country. I must admit that my introduction to this craft was terribly confusing. As an archaeologist, the drive to understand an ancient people was lost in the process we call science. It took years for me to begin to understand the differences between McElmo and Mesa Verde Black-on-white. Only when I realized that the process of classification was an arbitrary construct, was I able to see the ebb and flow of the continuity of Anasazi ceramics.

An alternative view of the Ancient Ones' pottery is purely esthetic. This approach is tempting because it takes little thought and less effort to attain a personal satisfaction. This turns a physical reality into an impenetrable shadow. Can this bring us closer to the people who fashioned the pottery? Perhaps.

Over twenty years of my life have been wrapped up in the study of Mesa Verde pottery, from scientific analysis to attempts at replication. The result has been both satisfying and frustrating. Satisfying because I believe I am able to obtain information from the fragments of the past that may help me understand an ancient culture. Frustrating because after twenty years of attempted replication, I have not been able to achieve what even an Anasazi child must have been able to accomplish. Anasazi pottery is both right and left brained; utilitarian and aesthetic.

Ted Oppelt is able to stand back from the topic and see both the substance and the illusion. Historically, Mesa Verde pottery has been presented in scientific as well as artistic ways, but this work is a masterful combination of both. Although Ted is not formally trained as an archaeologist, his contribution to the use of pottery by Southwestern archaeologists is already well established. Now he has taken on yet another challenge: to bring the science as well as the artistry of Mesa Verde pottery, and through it a glimpse into the lives of another culture, to the public as well as the archaeological profession. Ted reveals himself as neither a mystic nor a scientist. He takes both approaches and mixes them into a holistic presentation that does credit to both. I envy his ability to stand back; I am afraid, at times, I am too close.

Dr. Bruce Bradley
Crow Canyon Archaeological Center

ACKNOWLEDGMENTS

A number of persons have provided valuable assistance in the research reported in this book and in its preparation. Over the past five years, the staff at the Mesa Verde Research Center have been very helpful. Dr. Jack Smith, chief of the Research and Cultural Management Division, has provided advice and several photographs and has allowed his staff to help me in examining pottery, maps, and site reports in the Center. Bill Cruetz, Liz Bauer, and Nancy Harris willingly spent much time helping me find the pottery in the collection. Others at Mesa Verde National Park who have been of significant help are Linda Martin, Bev Cunningham, Don and Kathy Fiero, and Art Hutchinson. Mary O. Griffitts, a volunteer at Mesa Verde, answered questions about the geology and clays of the area. I would also like to thank Marilyn Colyer who provided insightful comments and suggestions based on her extensive knowledge of the natural and cultural resources of Mesa Verde.

Several staff members of the Crow Canyon Archaeological Center cooperated in the research reported in this book and suggested improvements in the manuscript. Mr. Paul Ermigiotti has been of invaluable assistance. Dr. Bruce Bradley wrote the foreword and after reading the first draft, made many helpful corrections and suggestions. Lou Matis participated in the experimental firings and in the many discussions about the pottery of the Anasazi. Dr. Doug Bowman, Ute Mountain Ute Tribal Park archaeologist, gave me the opportunity to examine sherds on the surface of a number sites in the tribal park in Mancos Canyon.

I am greatly indebted to all of the archaeologists who have studied the pottery of Mesa Verde over the years. Their work, as reported in the list of references, provided the basis for much of this book. As always my wife, Pat, has been of great help. Specifically, she did the plant drawings, posed for the photographs of pottery making, and helped me understand the natural resources of Mesa Verde.

POTTERY OF THE PREHISTORIC
GREATER SOUTHWEST

In order to understand and appreciate the prehistoric pottery of Mesa Verde it is necessary to have some familiarity with the prehistoric pottery of the greater Southwest. This large region encompasses nearly all of the state of Arizona, the portion of New Mexico west of the Pecos River, southern Utah, and the southwest corner of Colorado. It also extends south into the northern parts of the Mexican states of Chihuahua and Sonora (see Map 1). A chronology of the major periods and events in the prehistory and history of Mesa Verde is shown in Table 1.

Archaeologists have divided this region into three major prehistoric cultural territories and have focused their research efforts on the groups that occupied the area beginning about the time of the birth of Christ. Earlier peoples inhabited this region back to at least 10,000 B.C., but lacking pottery they are beyond the scope of this book. The three major prehistoric cultures of the Southwest are known as the Hohokam, Mogollon, and Anasazi. These cultures have been separated and identified by study of their material cultural remains, particularly the evidence provided by their distinctive types of pottery. The Hohokam lived in the south-central part of the present state of Arizona and adjacent northern Sonora, Mexico. To the east, the Mogollon inhabited the mountainous area of southwestern New Mexico, southeastern Arizona, and northern Chihuahua, Mexico. The largest portion of the greater Southwest was inhabited by the Anasazi. Their area extended over northern New Mexico west of the Pecos River, into southwestern Colorado, most of southern Utah, and northern Arizona south to the Little Colorado River (see Map 1). The proposed boundaries of these cultural areas are not precise; therefore, cultural materials, including types of pottery, may have been made and used in more than one cultural area. However, a major determinant of the extent of these three cultures has been the presence of certain types of prehistoric pottery.

It is not known where the first pot was made in the Southwest, but there is strong evidence that pottery making appeared first in the southern part of this region and then moved north by cultural diffusion. Because the earliest pottery in the Southwest is quite well made it is unlikely that it was independently developed in this region. The concept of pottery making

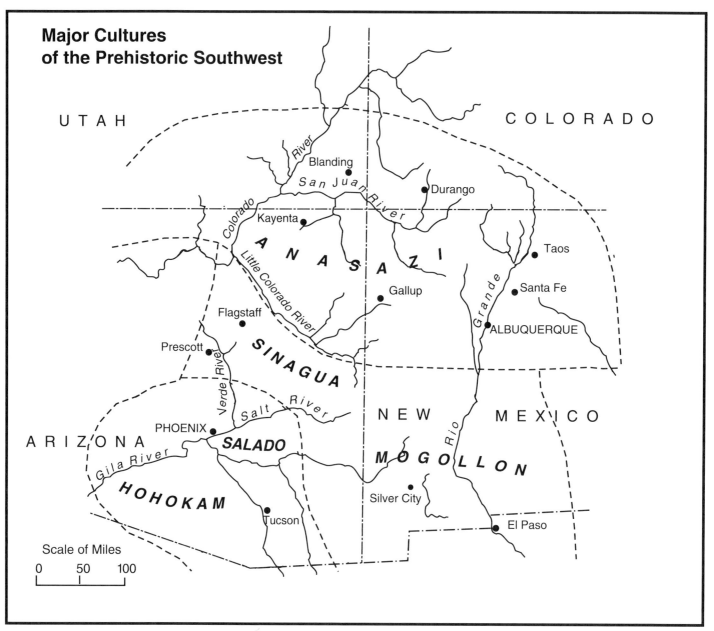

**Major Cultures
of the Prehistoric Southwest**

UTAH

COLORADO

Blanding

San Juan River

Durango

Colorado River

Kayenta

Taos

A N A S A Z I

Little Colorado River

Gallup

Santa Fe

Flagstaff

S I N A G U A

Grande

ALBUQUERQUE

Prescott

Verde River

Salt River

N E W

M E X I C O

PHOENIX

SALADO

Rio

ARIZONA

Gila River

M O G O L L O N

H O H O K A M

Silver City

Tucson

El Paso

Scale of Miles

0   50   100

Map 1

2

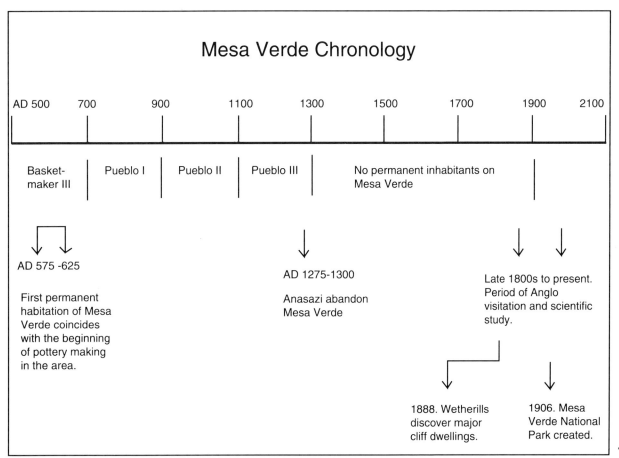

Table 1

probably came north from earlier potters in Mexico, although a dated sequence of pottery making has not yet been traced to its southern origins. Other significant cultural traits, such as the cultivation of maize, have been shown to have developed in Mexico and diffused north into the American Southwest.

The first southwestern pottery types, buff and red slipped wares (Vahki Plain and Vahki Red), appeared among the Hohokam of southern Arizona between A.D. 200 and A.D. 400. The later date is currently accepted by most researchers as more accurate. These earliest types precede the advent of pottery in the Mogollon and Anasazi areas. The first Mogollon pottery, a plain brown ware called Alma Plain, was made about the same time (circa A.D. 300) as Vahki Plain. The early contemporaneous Hohokam and Mogollon types differ in several significant technological characteristics. Although they were both built by coiling, the Hohokam ware was thinned and formed by the use of paddle and anvil, whereas the Mogollon pottery was finished by scraping. This significant difference in construction may indicate separate Mexican origins for these early Southwestern wares, although the specific Mexican sources of these two traditions are not known. The pottery thinned by scraping may have originated in the Loma San Gabriel culture of the Mexican states of Zacatecas and Durango (Kelley and Kelley, 1975), whereas the paddle-and-anvil construction among the Hohokam may have diffused along the west coast of Mexico from the early potters in Nayarit and Jalisco. The introduction of pottery making from south to north was probably by cultural diffusion from one group to the next rather than through an actual movement of populations. Representative types of Hohokam and Mogollon pottery are illustrated in Plates 1 and 2.

Although early unfired mudware has been found in the northern Southwest, the first true pottery in the Anasazi region is a brown ware (Rosa Brown) found in the Navajo Reservoir area of northwestern New Mexico and at a site in the Mancos Canyon south of Mesa Verde dated at A.D. 470. It is similar to the brown ware being made at that time in the Mogollon country to the south. It may have been made locally, but it seems more probable that it was traded in from the south. The first locally made gray pottery appeared circa A.D. 575, and supplanted the brown ware by the A.D. 600s. By the sixth century A.D. the early gray ware appeared throughout the Anasazi region. The advent of the gray ware tradition among the Anasazi in the late 500s represents the beginning of firing in a neutral or reducing atmosphere. The sedimentary clays used by the Anasazi potters encouraged the development of a new technique of reduction or neutral firing to produce the gray color. This method of firing cannot be traced to the Mogollon or Hohokam to the south. Further research may produce a source farther south in Mexico, but at present this seems to be one of the few true innovations of the early Anasazi potters (Breternitz, 1982).

The use of a light-colored slip to produce a smooth,

contrasting background on the surface of vessels is characteristic of both the early Hohokam red-on-buff wares and the Mogollon red-on-brown wares. The Anasazi adopted this concept by using white firing clay to produce an excellent white slip. In later centuries the Mogollon produced black-on-white by applying a white slip to oxidized fired brown ware. The Anasazi potters, using a clay with little iron, fired their pots in a reducing or neutral atmosphere and produced vessels that were often white throughout the walls of the vessel.

Although characteristics of decoration and temper varied from one Anasazi area to another, by the 600s similar gray wares with black mineral decorations were being produced throughout the Anasazi region. These first decorated types have been named Lino Black-on-gray and La Plata, or Chapin, Black-on-white.

In the 700s, neckbanding of gray ware culinary vessels appeared among the Anasazi, and in the 900s overall pinched corrugations on utility vessels became very popular. These two new methods of surface manipulation were probably diffused from the Mogollon to the south along the mountain trade route that approximates the present Arizona-New Mexico state line. Hatched designs adopted throughout the Anasazi region appeared in the 900s very soon after their advent in the Mogollon area.

Red wares (not the impermanent red wash) first appeared in the northern San Juan area in the 900s. This may have been an innovation of the Anasazi in southeastern Utah where it is the predominant ware in some sites on Alkali Ridge (Brew, 1946). Bill Lucius believes that these red wares are a variation of the reduction-fired gray ware tradition, and were reduced during most of the firing and oxidized in the final stage (Breternitz, 1982:135).

During the first seven centuries of pottery development among the Anasazi, the following similarities can be noted throughout the region:

- An initial gray ware made of sedimentary clays
- Firing with an initial reduction and a final oxidation
- Manufacture by the coil-and-scrape method
- Black-on-gray decoration followed by a slipped black-on-white
- Shapes and designs similar over broad areas during time periods (Breternitz, 1982)

Pinched surface corrugations were popular over a long period among both the Mogollon and Anasazi, but are absent in Hohokam pottery. This type of surface treatment is unique among prehistoric potters of the Southwest.

Considering the great variety of ways to produce a clay pot, production of pottery was remarkably similar over a large area for more than ten centuries. This reflects strong traditions and possible contact among the cultures and subcultures of the Southwest. There are local variations in materials, manufacture, and decoration, but there are more similarities than differences. All the pottery was hand formed and built by placing one coil upon another. Only the techniques of thinning and shaping—by either paddle and anvil or scraping—varied. Building by the use of slabs or molds was not used. The potter's wheel, which developed early in much of the world, was unknown. Although glazes were used as decorations from A.D. 1250 to 1680 in the Zuni and Rio Grande areas, they were never used to cover the entire vessel surface. Incising, punching, and cordmarking were common on prehistoric pottery of the Eastern and Plains peoples but were rare in the Southwest.

A true enclosed kiln was not used in the prehistoric Southwest. The few kiln areas reported in the northern San Juan are shallow firing pits. The only known true kilns in the New World were in the Gulf Coast region and the highlands of Mexico (Rice, 1987).

Among the three major prehistoric cultures of the Southwest there were variations in vessel shape, but within each culture during the later centuries, shapes became more standardized and eccentric vessels become scarce. This may have resulted from the development of strong pottery traditions in each culture.

A remarkable condition in the Greater Southwest is the documented two-thousand-year continuity of pottery making by prehistoric, historic, and contemporary potters. In spite of the four centuries of European domination and attempts to destroy the native culture, many Pueblo Indian potters are still producing beautiful wares with traditional materials and without kilns, wheels, or other nontraditional tools and methods.

This brief treatment of prehistoric pottery in the greater Southwest provides a background for the following description of the development of pottery making in one area of the Anasazi cultural region, the Mesa Verde (see Map 2).

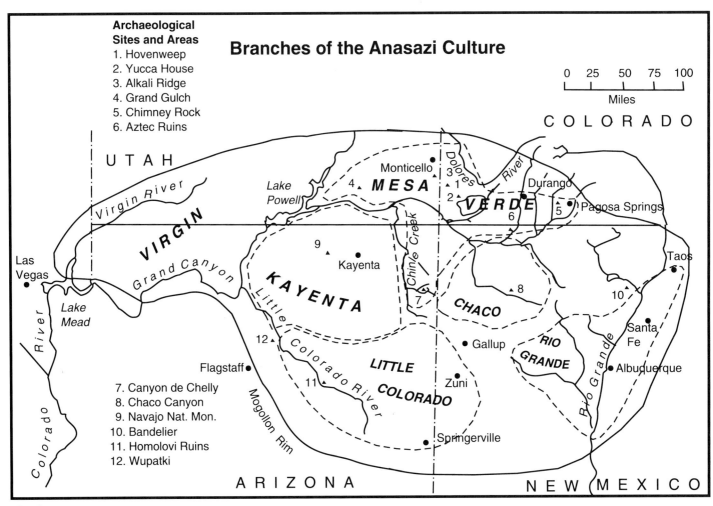

Archaeological
Sites and Areas
1. Hovenweep
2. Yucca House
3. Alkali Ridge
4. Grand Gulch
5. Chimney Rock
6. Aztec Ruins

Branches of the Anasazi Culture

0   25   50   75   100
Miles

COLORADO

UTAH

Lake
Powell

Monticello

MESA

VERDE

Durango

Pagosa Springs

Las
Vegas

Lake
Mead

VIRGIN

Virgin River

Grand Canyon

Colorado River

KAYENTA

Kayenta

Chinle Creek

CHACO

Taos

Santa
Fe

Albuquerque

Little Colorado River

12

11

Flagstaff

7. Canyon de Chelly
8. Chaco Canyon
9. Navajo Nat. Mon.
10. Bandelier
11. Homolovi Ruins
12. Wupatki

Mogollon Rim

LITTLE
COLORADO

Gallup

Zuni

RIO
GRANDE

Rio Grande

Springerville

ARIZONA

NEW MEXICO

Map 2

THE SIGNIFICANCE OF POTTERY IN THIRTEEN CENTURIES OF MESA VERDE HISTORY

Pottery is the most significant of the cultural remains left by the prehistoric inhabitants of Mesa Verde. In the fourteen centuries since the Basketmakers first settled on Mesa Verde, the local pottery has been of great importance to all of the permanent and temporary dwellers in this area.

The Prehistoric Era

During the latter part of the sixth century A.D., the Basketmaker peoples of the northern San Juan, around Mesa Verde, were increasingly relying on agriculture, particularly the cultivation of corn, as their means of subsistence. In earlier times, the gathering and hunting activities of these people made baskets the most practical type of portable container. Baskets were light, durable, and easily transported. The change from a hunting-gathering life to a more sedentary existence, dependent primarily on horticulture, brought about the need for different types of containers. The more permanent abodes of these people permitted them to use heavier, breakable vessels that were more efficient for cooking and food storage than were baskets. It is probable that the Anasazi in the southern part of their region acquired the knowledge of pottery making from the Mogollon people to the south, and then passed it on to the northern Anasazi in the Mesa Verde area (Breternitz, 1982). The advent of pottery making in the northern San Juan coincided with the movement of the Basketmakers from the surrounding valleys onto Mesa Verde, circa A.D. 575. As their proficiency in pottery making increased, their basketmaking skills declined. This can be seen by comparing the finely woven, decorated sandals of the Basketmakers with the relatively coarse, plain ones of the Pueblo III people. However, some finely made baskets were still produced.

Pottery soon became one of the most important aspects of the Mesa Verdeans' material culture. Its major functions were related to the preparation, serving, and storage of food, but as discussed later, pottery was also utilized in many other ways.

Pottery making also met the Anasazis' needs for artistic expression and for beautifying their surroundings. To the eyes of modern viewers, the beautiful black-on-white vessels of the Pueblo I–III potters are the most striking of these peoples' artistic remains. De-

Fig. 1a. Piedra Black-on-white gourd-shaped jar. Coyote Village, MVNP.

Fig. 1b. Piedra Black-on-white seed jar. Coyote Village, MVNP.

signs used on pottery were also used to decorate walls, weavings, and tools. The many uses of pottery made it nearly indispensable to the ancient inhabitants of Mesa Verde. It is probable that every person utilized pottery in one way or another each day of their lives. They certainly could have survived without pottery, but their lives would have been much different and more difficult without it.

The most precious commodity on Mesa Verde was, and still is, the scarce water. Lacking permanent streams or lakes, the Anasazi were totally dependent on rain and snow melt. The underlying porous sandstone formations served as a huge reservoir charging the springs and seeps, enabling the Anasazi to survive during the long periods between rains. Without this great underground holding capacity, they could not have survived on the sporadic fourteen to sixteen inches (35 to 40 cm.) of annual precipitation. The

transportation and storage of water was essential to life. The remains of several forms of pottery vessels used to transport and store water give evidence of the importance of these functions. Gourds and skins can be used to transport water, but pottery is more flexible in form and more efficient for short-term storage. It is interesting to note that some of the early Basketmaker and Pueblo I vessels were made in the shape of gourds, namely gourd-shaped jars and seed jars (Figures 1a and 1b).

The Era of Early Anglo Visitation

The early Anglo settlers in the late nineteenth century were initially most impressed by the great Pueblo III cliff dwellings, but as they began to search for artifacts they soon gained an appreciation for the striking Pueblo black-on-white pottery vessels. The large collections made by the Wetherill brothers and other early diggers were primarily composed of pottery. Although their efforts to obtain pottery and other artifacts destroyed valuable scientific data, they also had an indirect positive influence by publicizing Mesa Verde and the need to preserve it. The large collections from Mesa Verde made by the Wetherills were exhibited at the Columbian Exposition of 1893 in Chicago, which promoted concern for preserving these artifacts and their source. This publicity influenced public awareness of the need to preserve Mesa Verde and helped lead to its eventual designation as a national park in 1906.

This is not a justification for the pot hunting of the early visitors; rather, these activities should be viewed in light of the lack of understanding of the archaeological value of these remains a century ago. Fortunately, the advancement of understanding and appreciation for cultural remains has brought us to the present level of protection of Mesa Verde and other national parks and monuments containing remains of the Anasazi. Unfortunately, due to the lack of personnel and the attitudes of some local citizens, most of the other federal lands containing prehistoric resources, outside the national parks, are not well protected and are still being vandalized.

The early collectors of the late nineteenth century learned much about the remains of the Anasazi, and some, such as Earl H. Morris, became outstanding archaeologists. Thus, the early exploiters' interest in Mesa Verde, motivated to a great extent by the desire to obtain pottery, in the long term served to awaken the public and lawmakers to the need to protect and preserve Mesa Verde.

The Era of Scientific Study

The first scientific study of Mesa Verde and its pottery was conducted a century ago by Gustav Nordenskiold,

a young Swedish scientist. He accurately described the plain, corrugated, and painted wares including the type we now call Mesa Verde Black-on-white. Nordenskiold made suggestions about how the pottery was made, and examined the clay, temper, and paint of the pottery he found. Considering the level of scientific understanding of prehistoric pottery one hundred years ago, his conclusions are remarkably accurate. In 1893, Nordenskiold wrote:

> Among these objects there are none that bear witness to the attainment of proficiency in a fixed industry so clearly as the specimens of pottery. The ornamentation of the earthenware also betokens a certain sense of beauty, a quality which we have no opportunity of observing in other productions of the cliff-peoples' industry. (See pages 76–77.)

Since Nordenskiold's pioneering work, a great deal of study has been done of the prehistoric pottery of the Mesa Verde region, contributing much to our knowledge of Anasazi culture. In the early years of southwestern archaeology, there was much interest in the ubiquitous potsherds of this region. The importance of pottery to southwestern archaeology is emphasized in the words of Harold S. Colton, a leading pioneer in the study of the prehistoric Southwest:

> Except for stone tools, artifacts made of pottery are the most durable products of prehistoric life that the archaeologist has to work with, and because the clay is fluid in the hands of the potter, it expresses more than any other material the difference in human activity in time and space. (1953:73)

Colton devised a system for naming pottery types that was based on the binomial system of naming plants and animals. The first name reflects a geographical landmark such as a river, mesa, or town in the area in which the type is commonly found. The second name gives a brief description of an outstanding physical characteristic of the type. Thus, Chaco Black-on-white is a black-on-white pottery commonly found in the area of Chaco Canyon, New Mexico. It is important to note that the type names do not describe discrete types, and there is much overlap among types, particularly those based on subjective criteria such as designs.

The prehistoric pottery of Mesa Verde is of great value to archaeologists in understanding the Anasazi culture for several reasons:

- It is present at nearly all sites; there are only a handful of preceramic sites on Mesa Verde.
- In the dry climate of this area, it is practically indestructible.
- Its plasticity is sensitive to cultural changes of its makers.
- It reflects changes in both time and space.
- It is not valued in sherd form by most artifact collectors, and therefore is commonly left in place.
- It is easy to collect, handle, store, and study.
- Types can be dated by establishing their context in ruins previously dated by tree-rings.

Prehistoric pottery is widespread throughout the Greater Southwest, and has been intensively studied for many years. In addition to the Mesa Verde types described in Chapter Four, there are approximately 1,200 types of pottery in the Southwest (Oppelt, 1988). This large body of knowledge enables archaeologists to recognize intrusive pottery that indicates human interaction between areas of manufacture. Although not much intrusive pottery has been found in Mesa Verde, what is present provides information about the time of contacts or trade with other peoples. The abundance of pottery sherds in a refuse mound gives an indication of the population size, and the types present give clues to the period of occupation. The pottery forms present also indicate something about the diet and habits of the inhabitants.

The large amounts of prehistoric sherds and vessels curated at the Mesa Verde Research Center and other institutions throughout the Southwest hold much data for further studies and will lead to a better understanding of the prehistory of this area (Figure 2). Large vessel collections from some sites provide data for possible identification of individual potters, which could lead to better understanding of family organization and trade among neighboring communities. Careful examination of wear patterns on vessels can lead to understanding of their uses. These are only a few examples of how well-documented collections of pottery can be used to reconstruct prehistoric societies.

By careful excavation through layers of undisturbed refuse, the pottery types found at each level give a relative chronology of the site. This does not give absolute dates because the pottery sequence does not relate directly to the date of a known event, such as the birth of Christ. Fortunately, the use of tree-ring dating in the Southwest has enabled archaeologists to assign approximate absolute dates of manufacture to some pottery types (Breternitz, 1966). This was done by examining the tree rings in the construction beams to date a structure or context in which the pottery type was found. One set of dates is not sufficient to date a pottery type, but careful excavation of a number of sites often provides a range of dates that narrow the dates of manufacture for the pottery found at those sites. Another, less precise, method of dating a pottery type is cross-dating by relating the context of the undated type to dated types within the same context.

Fortunately, on Mesa Verde we have many usable tree-ring samples from the prehistoric sites. Therefore, the local pottery types can be accurately dated. The two main conditions necessary for accurate tree-ring dating are present in this area: (1) species of trees that grow a visible ring each year (i.e., Douglas Fir, Piñon Pine, and Utah Juniper); and (2) a dry climate that preserves wood for a long period of time. The dry climate of Mesa Verde also discourages insects that might contribute to the decomposition of wooden beams.

The climate in those cliff dwellings protected by overhangs is so dry that the timbers used to build them have been preserved for over seven hundred years. Although beams are less common in surface pithouse sites, burned pithouses provide much carbonized wood that can be accurately dated. The conditions described above have provided abundant tree-ring dates for an accurate chronological sequence on Mesa Verde, and have made it unnecessary to use less precise dating techniques.

The well-dated pottery types on Mesa Verde can be used to date sites that lack datable wood. A scatter of potsherds is the only surface indication of some buried sites. Such sites can be roughly dated by analyzing the dates of the pottery types present. Features such as burials, check dams, shrines, petroglyphs, and reservoirs can be assigned probable dates if dated pottery types are found in context with them. These uses indicate how valuable pottery is to the archaeological study of the prehistoric Anasazi of Mesa Verde. A detailed description of how researchers believe this pottery was made is presented in the next chapter.

Fig. 2. Pottery from Wetherill Mesa Project excavations, Douglas Osborne. (*Courtesy MVNP*)

ANASAZI POTTERY MANUFACTURE

Lacking firsthand knowledge of the methods and materials used by the ancient potters of Mesa Verde, we must rely on three other available sources of information. First, there is the ethnographic data supplied by the historic and present potters of the Rio Grande Pueblos and the Acoma, Zuni, and Hopi to the west. It is generally accepted that some of the residents of these Pueblos are descendants of the Mesa Verdeans who migrated to these areas in the late thirteenth century. Therefore, the pottery-making methods of the present traditional Pueblo potters are believed to be similar, although not identical, to those of their Anasazi ancestors.

The second source of information is the careful examination of the many prehistoric vessels and sherds excavated from sites at Mesa Verde. Analysis of this pottery has enabled us to learn much about the ancient potters' methods and materials. Visual examination can show how the vessels were made, and microscopic and chemical analyses can uncover characteristics of the clay, temper, and paint. Much valuable information remains to be obtained from the extensive collections at the Mesa Verde Research Center and at other institutions.

The third, and most recent, source of information are the replication experiments at the Crow Canyon Archaeological Center near Cortez, Colorado, and at the University of Colorado summer field sessions directed by Joe Ben Wheat at Yellow Jacket, Colorado. The analysis in this book is based in part on information presented in a 1989 paper by Bruce Bradley, entitled "Anasazi Pottery Making." During the summers of 1988 to 1990, three seasonal staff members at Mesa Verde National Park conducted experimental firings of vessels made from local materials. The information on pottery manufacture presented in this volume comes in part from these pilot studies. An excellent general source of information is the book *Pottery Analysis,* written by Prudence Rice in 1987. This book covers pottery made by native peoples throughout the world with much information pertaining to prehistoric pottery of the Southwest. Other important sources are *Archaeological Studies in the La Plata District* (Morris, 1939) and *Ceramics for the Archaeologist* (1965), both by Anna O. Shepard. These two publications provide much valuable information on the technology of prehistoric pottery of the northern San Juan area.

Materials

A logical beginning point in the discussion of prehistoric pottery making in Mesa Verde is to examine the materials used and the possible sources of these materials. Ethnographic observation, analysis of prehistoric pottery, and replication studies have all contributed to this section.

Clay

The clay used to form the gray and white wares comes from the carbonaceous shale lenses found in the sandstones of the Mesa Verde Formation or from the underlying Mancos shale. In the Montezuma Valley to the west, the shale layers are common in the Dakota Sandstone Formation. These clays are plastic and are not overly sensitive to shrinkage when subjected to extreme, sudden changes in temperature during firing. Another form of clay used is montmorillonite, a member of the smectite group of phyllosicates; it is formed by the alteration of basic rock and minerals or the decomposition of volcanic ash (Rice, 1987). There are other types of clay on Mesa Verde that could have been used, but they were not suitable to the Anasazi for white or light gray fired pottery.

Shepard (1939) states that the clay used in the La Plata area to the southeast to make the red wares was different from that used to make the gray and white wares, although it was locally available. The red wares found during the Dolores Archaeological Program to the north of Mesa Verde were all made of nonlocal materials (Breternitz, 1982). The clays used to make the red wares on Mesa Verde proper are visually different from those used in the gray or white wares, but microscopic or chemical analyses need to be done to determine the sources of this clay. All of the clays used to make local Mesa Verde pottery need further study to better understand the technology of pottery making in this area.

Temper

As are most clays in the Southwest, the natural clay on Mesa Verde is too plastic to fire without cracking. In order to prevent this, larger nonplastic particles, known as temper, must be added to the clay. The temper facilitates drying and firing, and increases thermal shock resistance (Rice, 1987). Temper can be made of a great variety of animal, plant, and mineral materials. On Mesa Verde the materials used were crushed igneous rock, crushed sandstone, sand, and crushed potsherds. Sandstone, sand, and potsherds are readily available on the Mesa, but igneous rock is scarce. The closest source of igneous cobbles is the Mancos River Canyon, several miles from most areas of habitation. There was a change during the seven centuries of prehistoric pottery making on Mesa Verde from predominantly crushed igneous rock temper in Basketmaker III pottery to crushed potsherds in Pueblo III. The simplest explanation for this change is the increased availability of potsherds around the habitation sites over the many years of pottery making. It was certainly easier to obtain in later periods than was igneous rock.

Temper material is important not only in the successful production of pottery, but it also can be used by archaeologists to determine the source of the pottery. The source of most clay is difficult to pinpoint, but the origin of the minerals in temper can sometimes be quite specifically determined. Some clays have naturally occurring nonplastic particles that serve as temper. The proportion and size of temper particles varies with the type of clay and possibly with the use of the pottery. Examination of Mesa Verde sherds shows that the proportion of temper to clay was higher and the particles larger in the gray ware intended for culinary use than in the white wares which were more commonly used as food serving vessels. This may be due to the fact that the larger temper particles served to protect the vessel from thermal shock in the rapid heating and cooling over cooking fires.

Further studies of the temper in different types and forms of Mesa Verde pottery may provide valuable information on the Anasazi of this area. As David Breternitz has pointed out, the answers to many questions concerning pottery of the northern San Juan (such as the origin of the red wares) will have to be based on occurrences and distribution of tempering materials (1982:144).

Slip

A slip is a thin fluid suspension of clay in water that is wiped or brushed onto the smoothed surface of a vessel prior to firing. The purpose of a slip is to provide a smooth, even-colored surface that contrasts better with the black painted design. The very white slip used by contemporary potters at Acoma and other pueblos may be made of white-firing kaolin clay. Kaolin-producing geologic formations are not present in Mesa Verde. The source of the white-firing slip clay used by the prehistoric Mesa Verde potters has not been located. It has been suggested this clay may have been traded in, but it is also possible that further study will reveal a local source of this material. It may also be that our unsuccessful attempts to produce a white surface are the result of our inability to control the atmosphere in an open bonfire.

Early white (actually gray) wares on Mesa Verde were not slipped, but by A.D. 750 to 800 a white slip was being applied to some of the vessels. During the Pueblo II and III periods nearly all of the white wares were slipped. This practice probably diffused north from groups of Anasazi in the south where white slips appeared as early as A.D. 600.

The term "wash" refers to impermanent color applied to the surface of a vessel after firing. The Basketmakers on Mesa Verde covered some Chapin Gray vessels with a red ochre wash. The vessels with this wash are known as Fugitive Red (Plate 3).

Paint

As indicated in the later pottery type descriptions, mineral and organic pigments, and sometimes both, were used to decorate the prehistoric pottery of Mesa Verde. The earliest decorated types have predominantly mineral paint. This paint was obtained by crushing and grinding naturally occurring nodules or concretions of iron, or less commonly, manganese. The crushed minerals were mixed with water and applied to the surface of the pot. It may be, however, that because mineral paint did not adhere well to vessel surfaces, it was sometimes mixed with an organic medium made of boiled plant juices. Thus, some pottery on Mesa Verde has paint with both mineral and organic constituents.

The organic paint used by contemporary Pueblo potters is obtained by boiling young stems of the Rocky Mountain beeweed (Cleome sp.) until a dark green residue of carbon remains. This is dried and stored in cakes that can later be soaked in water to produce an organic paint. Rocky Mountain beeweed is now scarce on Mesa Verde, but it is found in Rock Canyon in the southwest corner of Mesa Verde National Park (Figure 3). Another plant, tansy mustard (Descurania pinnata), is more common on Mesa Verde and could have been used to make organic paint. In order to obtain a good black color from organic paint, the firing must be well controlled. If the fire is completely oxidized the carbon will be burned off leaving only a faint gray shadowy design. If mineral paint is fired in a fully oxidized atmosphere, the iron in the paint will turn red, and body clay with iron will fire to a buff color (Plate 4). Poorly fired white ware on Mesa Verde sometimes exhibits these colors. The potters of the Pueblo III period on Mesa Verde sometimes combined mineral and carbon paint on a pot to produce a variety known as Mesa Verde Polychrome (Figure 4), which is described in the next chapter.

The painted red wares on Mesa Verde have a red mineral paint made of iron (specular hematite) in the earlier types. In the later red ware, Deadmans Black-on-red, a blacker paint with a purple tinge is made of manganese.

The paint on most sherds can be visually identified (Plate 4). A few sherds with faint or badly weathered paint require thermal or chemical analysis to separate the mineral-painted sherds from those with carbon paint. The following characteristics are useful in visually identifying paint on sherds from Mesa Verde (a 10X lens is helpful in determining some of these features):

Color. Both carbon (organic) paint and mineral paint can give a good black color, but in a partially oxidizing fire the carbon paint tends toward gray, whereas the mineral paint becomes a reddish brown.

Physical state. Carbon paint is partially absorbed into the surface of the vessel; it is therefore similar in smoothness and luster to the unpainted portions. It shows no relief on the surface. Mineral paint coats the surface, often producing a slight relief above the surrounding surface. The texture and luster of mineral paint is independent of the unpainted areas.

Edges of lines. The edges of carbon-painted designs may be blurred or hazy because it diffuses into the surface. The edges of mineral paint designs are usually even and sharp.

Paint. The denseness of carbon paint is often uneven, with the center of wide lines lighter than the edges. Mineral paint may be sintered (bumpy) or slightly vitrified (nearly melted) producing a gritty glaze-like surface.

Tools

Prehistoric pottery-making tools were made from a variety of natural materials. Examination of tools found in sites, observation of modern Pueblo potters, and ex-

perimentation in pottery making provide the following descriptions of these instruments.

Brushes

The brushes used by the Anasazi potters to apply the decorations have not survived, but they were probably made from the broad-leafed yucca plant (Figure 5). Many contemporary Pueblo potters still use yucca brushes. They are easily made by soaking yucca leaves in water to soften them and then cutting them

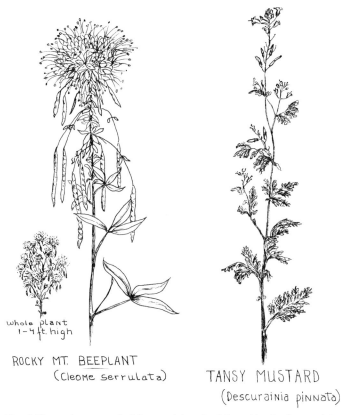

whole plant
1–4 ft. high

ROCKY MT. BEEPLANT
(Cleome serrulata)

TANSY MUSTARD
(Descurainia pinnata)

Fig. 3 Two plants probably used by the Mesa Verde Anasazi to produce organic (carbon) paint for decorating pottery. (*Drawing by Pat Oppelt*)

Fig. 4. Mesa Verde Black-on-white bowl with polychrome exterior decoration. Mug House, MNVP. (*Courtesy MVNP*)

Fig. 5. Broad-leafed yucca, (Yucca bacata). MVNP.

Fig. 6. Pottery making tools. *Upper row*: Sherd scrapers. *Middle row*: Polishing stones. *Lower row*: Yucca paint brushes.

Fig. 7. Basket impressions on exterior of Mancos Black-on-white bowl.

into four- to five-inch sections. One end of each section is scraped or chewed to free the strong yucca fibers that form the bristles (Figure 6). Modern brushes of this type often have long bristles that enable the painter to paint fine, straight lines on the surface of the vessel. Slips are usually applied by wiping with the fingers or with a wad of rabbit fur.

Scrapers

All Anasazi pottery was made by the coil-and-scrape method; therefore, pottery scrapers were an integral part of the potter's tool kit. Although the surface of some gray ware vessels show evidence of the use of scrapers made from potsherds, an examination of worked sherds in the collections of the Mesa Verde Research Center shows few worked sherds that could have been used to scrape pottery (Figure 6). Pieces of gourd rind with smoothed edges were probably commonly used by the Anasazi to scrape their pots. The Pueblo potters of today use gourd rinds and many other materials to scrape their pottery vessels.

Polishing Stones

Later types of white and red wares made on Mesa Verde were usually polished to produce a smooth, lustrous surface. The polishing was done by rubbing a smooth, hard stone back and forth over the surface. In order to work well these stones must be of a fine-grained texture, such as andesite, that has been smoothed by natural processes or use (Figure 6). Few pebbles on Mesa Verde are naturally smooth enough to serve as polishing stones. Therefore, well-used polishing stones were prized tools of the ancient potters and were probably passed down from a potter to her descendants. A variety of shapes are needed to polish the various curvatures and tight places on the vessels. Dinosaur gizzard stones (gastroliths) that have been ground smooth by the dinosaur's digestive processes

make good polishing stones. These are not common on Mesa Verde, but are found in the Morrison Formation in McElmo Canyon to the west.

Pot Forms

Most prehistoric vessels made on Mesa Verde have round bases. In order to form such a base the vessel must be supported while in its plastic state, or the weight of the pot will flatten the base. Pot forms of several types were used to support the vessel during forming. In the early period of pottery making on Mesa Verde, stiff, shallow baskets were used for this purpose. The impressions of basket coils are present on the exteriors of some Basketmaker III and Pueblo I bowls (Figure 7). Later pot forms were commonly made of large potsherds with ground edges. These are sometimes called *pukis*, a word from the Tewa language spoken by the people in several of the Pueblos of the northern Rio Grande. A few ground sherds that could have served as pot forms have been found on Mesa Verde (Figure 8). Thick woven rings of yucca fibers were used to support round-bottomed vessels on the floor or while being carried on the head (Figures 9 and 10). These woven pot rings may also have been used along with a sherd to support a pot while it was being formed. In addition to providing support, pot forms also facilitate turning the vessel during construction. This is especially useful in the forming of a very large vessel such as a water olla. Some prehistoric vessels on Mesa Verde have indented bases. Bruce Bradley notes that the curved surfaces of indented bases produce a strong base and a flat surface contact (Bradley, p.c. 1990).

Clay Preparation

The clay undoubtedly used by the Anasazi potters for white and gray wares was from the carbonaceous shale from the underlying Mancos shale or from shale

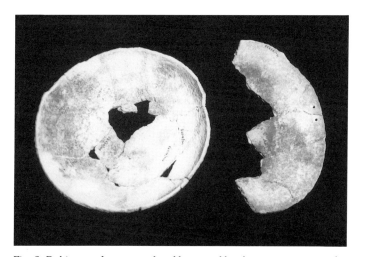

Fig. 8. Pukis: pot forms made of bases of broken pottery vessels.

Fig. 9. Twilled pot rest. Colorado State Museum. (*Courtesy MVNP*)

lenses found in the sandstones of the Mesa Verde formation. These clays are found in many places near the prehistoric habitation sites on Mesa Verde. There are shale layers within some of the alcoves utilized by the Anasazi of Pueblo III times, such as Long House and Balcony House. Weathered shale was probably preferred to the hard consolidated form. Crushing and grinding the latter on a metate is a time consuming job. It is possible to dissolve pieces of unground weathered shale in water, but the clay produced is lumpy and nonhomogeneous. The shale was collected in a basket or hide and the larger impurities removed by hand. The clay was then ground with a mano on a metate to a fine powder and cleaned further by hand or by winnowing on a breezy day. Some historic potters used the latter method by placing a cloth downwind and casting handfuls of dry clay into the air. The lighter particles of clay are carried by the wind onto the cloth while the larger, heavier particles and impurities drop near the potter's feet. This grinding, cleaning, and sorting prepares the clay for the addition of temper.

Fig. 10. Woven head ring for carrying pottery jar. Echo House, MVNP. (*Courtesy MVNP*)

If sand is to be used for temper, it is collected and then cleaned and sorted by hand to retain particles of the correct size. Igneous rock or potsherds must be crushed and ground with a mano on a metate and sifted or reground several times to the correct fineness. If the particles of temper are too large or numerous, the clay will lack plasticity causing the pot to crack or slump during formation. Conversely, particles that are too small or sparse will cause cracking during firing.

It is unlikely that the ancient potters needed to measure the proportion of temper to body clay. They probably used their experience with the color or feel of the mixture to judge the right proportion. Ethnographic observation and examination of potsherds indicate that the proportion by volume of temper to clay vary from 1:2 to 1:3. The proportion also varies from one type of clay to another. Some clays from other areas need no added temper; these are referred to as "self-tempered." An example of this is the clay used by the Taos potters in the northern Rio Grande area which contains numerous flakes of mica.

All of the clay used by the prehistoric potters on Mesa Verde appears to have temper added. After the temper was added, the dry ingredients were carefully mixed. A pile of tempered clay was then placed on a hide or in a large bowl and water was gradually added as it was mixed. If too much water was added, the clay was difficult to form and it was set out to dry. Experienced potters knew by feel when the clay was moist enough. Some modern Pueblo potters pinch a small ball of clay to determine its moisture content. If it cracks it needs more water.

The wet clay was then kneaded or wedged by hand or with the bare feet to eliminate air pockets, randomize the temper particles, and uniformly distribute the water. When the clay was prepared it was wrapped in a wet hide or placed in a moist bowl to cure. The clay was left for at least a few days and could be stored in-definitely if it was kept moist. The growth of bacteria in clay seems to improve its workability. Like some modern potters, prehistoric potters may have added something to promote fermentation in the clay.

Forming the Vessel

As previously noted, all Anasazi pottery was made by the coil-and-scrape method. This method is particularly effective in the production of large vessels such as ollas, used for water storage (Rice, 1987). The prehistoric potters of the New World did not develop a potter's wheel, so all of their pottery was hand formed except for a few molded wares in Mesoamerica.

There are several distinct ways to make a clay pot. The following, I believe, is how this was done by the Anasazi potters of Mesa Verde.

Pinch Pots

Small pots, those less than three or four inches in diameter, were made by the pinch pot method. A handful of clay was rolled into a ball between the palms of the hands. The thumbs were pushed into the clay to start the interior. Careful pushing and pinching around the sides thinned the walls and produced the desired shape. If a closed jar form was desired, the upper part of the walls were smoothed and contracted. To form a bowl, the walls were expanded. The fingers were moistened with water to smooth the walls and to prevent clay from sticking to the fingers. The walls may have been smoothed with a scraper, but these tiny vessels were rarely polished. If a painted decoration was desired, it was applied in the manner described later for larger vessels. A skilled potter could make a small pinch pot in a few minutes. The forming and decorating of miniature vessels was usually less carefully executed than the larger products. It has been speculated that these small pots were made by children who were learning the potter's craft, or that they were made for children as toys. It is interesting to note that, on Mesa Verde, miniature pots are more common in the Basket-maker III types (Chapin Gray and Chapin Black-on-white), than in the Pueblo III black-on-white or corrugated types (Figure 12). Unfired miniature pots are found in some Pueblo II and III sites.

Coiling and Scraping

The coil-and-scrape method used to make all of the larger Mesa Verde vessels began in one of two ways: a concave, circular slab of clay was formed between the palms to make the vessel base, or a coil of clay was used to begin a tight spiral at the center of the base (Figure 11a). Most white ware pots, and all of the corrugated ones, were started in the latter manner. If the slab method was used to start a round-bottomed vessel, it was placed in a sherd *puki* or shallow basket form sprinkled with ashes to prevent the clay from sticking. The slab was then pressed into the form to squeeze out any air bubbles. If bubbles remained anywhere in the wall of the pot they sometimes burst during firing. Some vessels have a slight indentation around the circumference on the lower part of the wall that was formed by the edge of the pot form pressing on the soft wall during construction (Figure 13). The edges of the base slab were then pulled up to form a low, vertical-wall base. The bases of the flat-bottomed mugs were usually made from a circular slab on a flat surface. Coils were then placed around the circumference of the base and bonded to it. An exception to this is one unusual mug examined by the writer that has a spiraled corrugated base. The spiraled corrugated bases of the round-bottomed corrugated vessels may have been dried in an inverted position to become firm so that the vessel weight would not flatten the soft coils.

After the base slab or spiral for a round-bottomed vessel was formed, a coil of clay was formed by rolling between the palms. These coils were usually slightly longer or shorter than the circumference of the vessel. The lengths were different than the vessel circumference so that the seams would not occur in the same place and thus weaken the pot. The thickness of the coils used varied with the size of the vessel and the preference of the potter. Most modern Pueblo potters use thick coils varying from half an inch to an inch in diameter to build their pots. Examination of prehistoric vessels and sherds from Mesa Verde shows that the coils used were significantly smaller in diameter. They were often only slightly larger than the thickness of the vessel walls. This is most easily seen in corrugated vessels. The potters probably varied the thickness of the coils depending on the plasticity of the clay used, the size of the pot, and the type of surface finish.

The first coil was placed on the upturned edge of the base slab. Each successive coil was then placed on the previous one, but not directly on top. The coils were slightly overlapped to strengthen the joints between them. This overlapping increased the surface contact area between the coils. If the circumference was being decreased to form the upper wall of a jar, each coil was placed on the interior edge of the preceding one. If the pot was being expanded to form a bowl, the coil was pinched onto the exterior edge of the preceding coil. Careful bonding of the coils was very important because weak bonds cracked during firing or use. Each coil was pinched down over the previous one to improve the bond. During Basketmaker III through the Pueblo I times, coils were usually layered in concentric circles, but in the later Pueblo II and III eras each coil was joined to the end of the previous one, forming a spiral (Figure 11b).

Little water was used during the joining process because too much moisture would weaken the vessel walls. Only enough water was used on the fingers to keep them from sticking to the clay (Bradley, 1989). After three or four coils were added, they were scraped

Fig. 11a. Two methods of starting a vessel base. *Left*: A concave slab. *Right*: A spiraled coil.

Fig. 11b. Adding concentric coils to form the wall of a bowl.

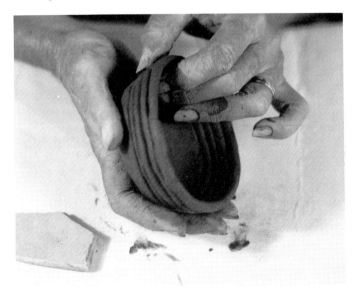

Fig. 11c. Pinching the coils to bond them.

Fig. 11d. Scraping the exterior of a bowl to smooth the surface and bond the coils.

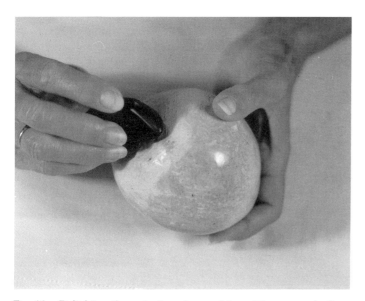

Fig. 11e. Polishing the exterior of a seed jar with a smooth, fine grained stone.

Fig. 11f. Painting the interior of a bowl with a fine Yucca brush.

before they dried. With the thin coils used by the Anasazi potters, scraping served a somewhat different function than it does with the thick coils of the modern Pueblo potters. The Anasazi potters scraped their wares primarily to smooth and bond; little clay was removed or redistributed. The ancient potters formed the basic shape during the coiling with the thin coils. In modern Pueblo pottery, the thick coils do not produce the final shape but are laid up in a cylindrical or slightly flared shape. It is the scraping that removes and redistributes the clay giving the vessel its finished shape. Thus, in shaping the pot, coiling or building was the primary process for the prehistoric potters, whereas the scraping is the most critical process in shaping the modern Pueblo vessels. Modern Acoma potters often flatten the coil before they apply it to the vessel.

It was important in using the thin coils that they not be allowed to become too dry before they were scraped. If they dried too much, the scraping would not adequately bond the coils. Another important aspect of the coil-and-scrape method was that during the scraping process counter pressure had to be applied to the vessel wall opposite the point being scraped. If this was not done, the wall was weakened and the coils poorly bonded. Today, larger vessels are built in stages because the weight of the upper vessel walls can cause the lower plastic walls to slump. The thin coils of the Anasazi pots may have made this less of a problem.

In the scraping process, a piece of gourd rind or a potsherd scraper was rubbed over the vessel to smooth the surface and bond the coils (Figure 11d). The hand not holding the scraper was used to apply counter pressure opposite the point being scraped. Scraping could be done in a number of ways, but experience and a skillful touch were needed to obtain the desired results. Some of the smoothing strokes were diagonal to the coils to improve bonding. Usually, both the interior and exterior of the vessel were scraped. In

Fig. 12. Miniature vessels. *Top row left to right*: bowl made of Mancos Black-on-white dipper, Chapin Black-on-white bowl, Mancos Black-on-white dipper bowl. *Bottom row left to right*: Chapin Gray seed jar, Chapin Gray "bird" jar, Mancos Black-on-white dipper, fragment of black-on-white pinch bowl. (Diameter of top middle vessel is 3⅝.")

Fig.13. Chapin Gray pitcher, pot form impression on lower base.

Fig. 14. Moccasin Gray rim sherds showing unobliterated neck coils.

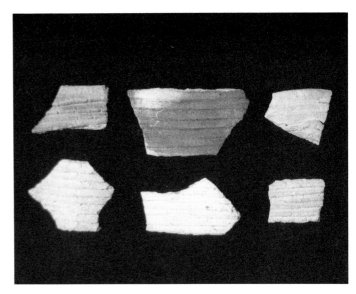

Fig. 15. Mancos Gray sherds. *Upper row*: Overlapping coils. *Lower row*: Tool-grooved coils.

Plate 1
Hohokam pottery vessels of several types.

Plate 2
Mogollon pottery vessels of several types.

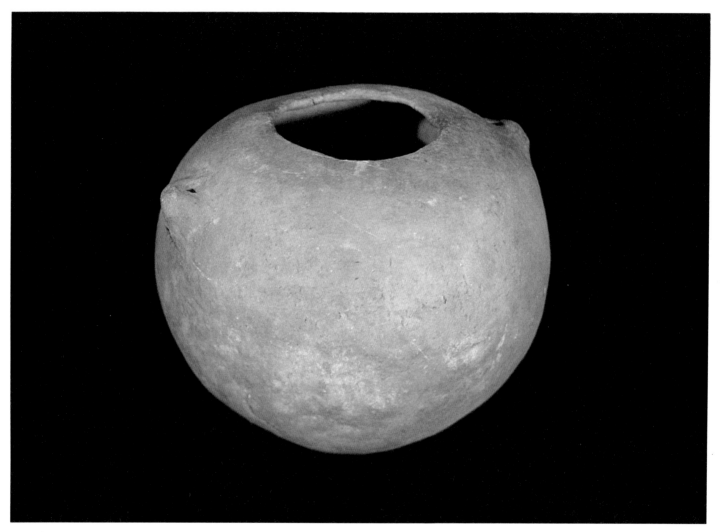

Plate 3
Fugitive Red seed jar.

Plate 4
Types of paint. *Upper row*: mineral paint. *Middle row*: organic (carbon) paint. *Lower row*: oxidized mineral paint.

Plate 5
Modern corrugated pitcher by "Sky" and corrugated seed jar by Stella Shutiva, Acoma Pueblo.

Plate 6
Chapin Black-on-white bowls.

tight areas, such as the inside of small jar necks and around handle attachment points, smoothing was difficult and unobliterated coils are often evident. Modern Pueblo potters usually scrape the interior first. Only enough water is used during scraping to keep the scraper from "grabbing" the clay (Bradley, 1989).

Surface Manipulations

In prehistoric Mesa Verde pottery from A.D. 900 to 1300, and at about the same time elsewhere in the Anasazi region, a distinctive surface manipulation was employed. This technique is known as "corrugation" or "neckbanding" in its earliest form. The first neck-banded type, known as Moccasin Gray, appeared about A.D. 750. This type and the succeeding neckbanded types are described in Chapter Five. Moccasin Gray was made by scraping the interior in the usual manner, but on the neck the coils were only flattened (Figure 14). A second type, Mancos Gray, is similar, except that the unobliterated coils were narrower and often not flattened. Sometimes the neck coils were accentuated by grooving the coil junctures with a pointed tool (Figure 15). Mummy Lake Gray, the final neckbanded type, had a single neckband below the rim made in a different manner (Figure 16). After the vessel was formed, but was still in the plastic state, a wide strip of clay was added to the finished rim below the lip.

The fully corrugated types made on Mesa Verde during Pueblo II and III times, Mancos Corrugated and Mesa Verde Corrugated, were made in the same manner. As each coil was placed on the preceding one, the interior was smoothed and bonded in the usual manner, but on the exterior the coil was pinched on around the vessel to produce regular indentations on the surface. Fingerprints and fingernail marks made in the soft clay appear in some indentations, indicating the technique used to form the corrugations. However, some of the indentations on the narrow coils are so fine that

Fig. 16. Mummy Lake Gray sherds showing single fillet below rim.

they may have been pressed with a small tool. Surface patterns on some Pueblo III corrugated vessels were formed by interspersing bands of plain coils within the indented areas (Figure 17). Other embellishments were produced by using a pointed tool to punch or incise a design on the corrugated surface or by running the fingertip over the soft clay to form shallow diagonal grooves.

Stella Shutiva and other potters of Acoma Pueblo produce modern copies of prehistoric corrugated wares by indenting the soft coils with a triangular-shaped tool, or less commonly by pinching the soft coils with the fingers or smoothing the surface and then finger-indenting the surface. A few non-Indians have mastered the formation of even corrugations; Plate 5 shows a pitcher and seed jar made by modern potters.

Rim Finishing

After the desired body shape was attained, the rim was finished and any needed handles attached. It is difficult to produce a strong, even rim on a hand-formed pot. Modern replicators have developed a technique that may also have been known to the Mesa Verdeans: one coil beyond the desired height of the vessel is bonded in the usual manner, and the edge of a scraper is then run around the rim of the vessel, using direct downward pressure to compress the clay and achieve the desired height. This produces a rim of excess clay on both the interior and exterior edges of the rim. The excess on both edges is carefully trimmed off with a sharp tool using a downward cutting stroke parallel to the wall of the vessel. If done correctly, this results in a strong, even slightly thickened rim. As in other stages, it is important not to add too much water to the rim (Bradley, 1989).

Fig. 17. Mesa Verde Corrugated jar with spirals of deep corrugations from rim to base. Long House, MVNP. (*Courtesy MVNP*)

Handles

Examination of broken-handled Anasazi pots shows that the handles of mugs, pitchers, ollas, bowls, and dippers were usually attached by a "riveting" process described by Bruce Bradley (1989). The handle was made of a flat strap or round coil slightly longer than the handle needed. The clay was trimmed at each end to form short tabs in the center of each end of the handle. The leather-hard vessel walls were carefully prepared by cutting two holes about the diameter of the handle tabs at the points of attachment. Then the handle was bent to the desired shape. Care had to be taken not to cause cracks beyond the inevitable surface cracks in the outer side. The handle tabs were carefully inserted into the holes in the vessel wall. As the end of the handle was held firmly in place against the vessel wall with one hand, the soft protruding end of the tab was squashed flat to produce a tight "rivet head" on the interior of the pot. The point of attachment was sometimes strengthened by forming a short, very thin coil of clay which was wrapped around the handle at its juncture with the exterior wall of the vessel. This coil was then pressed into the angle between the handle and the wall and smoothed to thicken and strengthen the attachment point.

Dipper handles presented a different problem because they had only one point of attachment. Solid dipper handles were usually circular or oblong in cross section and were attached to the bowl in the riveting manner described above. Pueblo III dippers often have hollow handles. These were attached by a "welding" process in which a small knob of clay was pinched up on the soft bowl exterior at the point of attachment. The end of the still-plastic hollow handle was pressed over the knob and against the wall of the bowl. This method of attachment was sometimes strengthened by pressing a small coil of clay between the handle and bowl wall, as in the riveting method.

Careful examination of broken dipper handles reveals another method of attachment of hollow handles (and perhaps solid handles as well). While the clay of the dipper bowl was still soft, deep random incisions were made on the exterior over the area of the handle attachment. When the soft end of the handle was pressed into this area, some of the clay entered the incisions, strengthening the bond between the handle and bowl.

An interesting variation in the attachment of hollow dipper handles among the Anasazi of the Kayenta branch is known as the phallic attachment. A short, solid cylindrical projection was attached to the dipper bowl in the riveted manner. This formed the male portion. A hollow tubular handle was formed with an interior diameter the same as the diameter of the male section. When the male and female parts had dried enough to be firm, but were still plastic, the male part was inserted into the hollow handle until the end of the handle met the dipper wall. The handle was then squeezed to bond the two parts together (Gratz, 1976).

Hollow handles were formed in two ways. A thin flat rectangular slab of clay was rolled so its long edges met and overlapped slightly. They were then bonded by pinching and smoothing to form a hollow tube. The second method was similar except that the slab of clay was wrapped around a cylindrical core of vegetable matter (for example, a roll of corn husks), which was left inside the handle. When the dipper was fired, the vegetable matter burned out leaving a hollow tubular handle. Plant stems may have been used in a similar manner to produce the small holes running through the stem of pottery pipes.

Hollow handles and thick solid handles often had small holes pierced through them before they hardened (Figure 18). This may have served to assure a more even firing of the handle interior. Small pellets of clay were placed inside some hollow handles to produce a rattling sound when they were shaken. The

Fig. 18. Mesa Verde and McElmo Black-on-white ladles. Lower shows holes through handle. (*Courtesy MVNP*)

writer has also examined one Mesa Verde Black-on-white mug with such a rattle handle. A few handles were made by bonding two or more unsmoothed coils together to form a band. The ends of these coil handles were attached to the pot in the riveting manner (Figure 19).

33

Fig. 19. Handle formed of two unsmoothed coils on Mesa Verde Black-on-white mug.

Very small lug handles, common on early Mesa Verde Gray vessels, appear to have been made by pinching up a small protrusion on the surface of a soft pot (Figure 20). Larger, more circular lug handles were formed by pushing a small ball of wet clay against the soft surface of a vessel, and then squashing the edges down to form a sloping attachment. These lugs were sometimes pierced while wet to form holes for suspension or left unpierced to aid in lifting the jar. A variety of jar, bowl, dipper, pitcher, and mug handles is illustrated in Figures 20 and 21.

Appliques applied to some Pueblo III jars, and less commonly to Pueblo I and II vessels, were formed of short thin coils of soft clay pressed onto the wet surface of the pottery. The most common form of applique was a small scroll placed on the neck of some Mesa Verde and Mancos Corrugated jars (Figures 22 and 51).

Surface Finishing

In the Basketmaker III era little effort was expended in finishing the surfaces of pottery vessels. As the centuries passed, however, the Mesa Verde potters devoted an increasing amount of time and care to this process. While the pot was still soft, the finishing and smoothing began. This was done by carefully scraping the surface to make it smoother and more regular. The better the scraping was done, the easier and more effective the polishing was. Large depressions on the surface were filled by pressing on small patches of clay. These had to be carefully bonded and smoothed to remove all air bubbles to prevent spalling during the firing.

The smooth lustrous surface on the later Mesa Verde white ware was produced during the polishing process. Today many Pueblo potters allow their pots to dry after forming, and then use sandpaper to sand the surface smooth and apply the slip to the dry vessel. They then polish over the slip. The early prehistoric potters on Mesa Verde usually used a different technique. After the surface was scraped to make an even,

Fig. 20. Vessel handles. *Upper row*: Loop jar handles, Chapin Gray and Mancos Black-on-white. *Middle row*: Loop bowl handles and two round lug canteen handles. *Lower row*: Pierced and unpierced lug bowl handles.

Fig. 21. Vessel handles. *Upper row*: Solid and hollow dipper handles. *Middle row*: Flat dipper handle, mug handle, pitcher handle and dipper handle. *Lower row*: Flat solid and round hollow dipper handles.

Fig. 22. *Upper row*: Applique coils on Mesa Verde Corrugated jars. *Lower row (left)*: Yucca twine in mending hole; *(middle)*: Basket impressions on bowl exterior; *(right)*: Painted design on rim interior of corrugated jar.

regular base, but was still damp, it was polished with a smooth, hard stone (Figure 11e). The pressure of polishing forced the larger particles of clay and temper down into the vessel wall and brought the finer particles to the surface, aligning them to produce a smooth, shiny surface. To achieve the desired effect, the clay had to be just wet enough. If the surface was too wet, the clay would catch on the polishing stone, but if it was too dry the rearrangement of the clay particles would not occur. Because the thin edges and protrusions on the pots dried more rapidly, they were ready to polish before the thicker sections. For this reason, polishing was usually done in several stages on different parts of the vessel. Polishing was a skill that took time to perfect. It was done by using short back and forth strokes with just the correct pressure over the entire surface. The surface had to be covered a number of times to obtain a good polish.

With the advent of organic paint on Mesa Verde,

about A.D. 1050, the ancient potters began polishing over the painted designs to produce a glossy finish on both the painted and unpainted areas. Some modern Pueblo potters are particularly skilled at this technique and polish pots for other potters who form and paint the vessels. This cooperative work in pottery making is common in some Pueblos, and it is likely the prehistoric potters followed this practice. Careful examination of the surface of prehistoric pots will reveal the almost invisible marks produced by the polishing stone. Polishing around small tight areas near rims and handles was very tricky. If the vessel had not hardened enough, too much pressure would crack the rim or break off a handle. The technique of counter pressure, like that used during the scraping process, helped prevent serious accidents. Deep cracks that formed during polishing could be cosmetically covered, but they were still present and would cause weak spots that might cause the pot to break during firing.

Slipping

Beginning sometime between A.D. 750 and 800 on Mesa Verde, a white slip was applied to the surface of most Mesa Verde White Ware vessels. Nearly all Cortez Black-on-white pieces have a good white slip, while Mancos Black-on-white bowl exteriors were sometimes left unslipped. On later types, all surfaces except the interior of jars were slipped. Slipping produced the even, white or pearl gray background typical of Pueblo II and Pueblo III pottery made on Mesa Verde. The slip was made of a fine fluid suspension of a white firing clay. Slip was applied in a liquid form with a brush or wad of cloth or animal fur, or as a paste applied with the fingers. The latter technique produced a thick slip that often formed a network of fine cracks during firing. Modern potters sometimes use five or six thin coats of slip to attain the correct coverage. For some clays, it was necessary to apply liquid slip before the vessel was completely dry. If a watery slip was applied to a dry pot, the rapid absorption would cause the pot to crack. The moisture that remained in partially dry vessels slowed the absorption and prevented cracking. After the slip had dried, some vessels were polished again.

It is sometimes difficult to determine whether or not a prehistoric sherd or vessel has been slipped. If a different clay of a contrasting color was used as a slip, its presence is obvious from examining the broken edge of a sherd. But, if the clay used for the slip was the same as that used for the body, and if it was applied in a thin, even coat, it is difficult to detect its presence, even with a microscope. The thick slip applied to Mesa Verde White Ware of the Pueblo III period developed a network of fine surface cracks known as crackling when it was fired (Figure 23). The cracks were caused by the differential expansion between the body clay and slip during drying and firing.

After a pot was slipped, it had to be completely dried. It was important that it not be dried too rapidly, or it would develop cracks. The initial drying was done in a shaded place away from drafts. After a few days it could be dried further in the sun or near some other source of heat. On Mesa Verde ten days of drying is sufficient for most vessels, with a longer time required for thicker vessels.

Painting

After the vessel was slipped, polished, and fully dried, the final step before firing was applying the painted design. If mineral paint was to be used it was preferred to have the surface slightly damp. This prevented the paint from being absorbed too quickly, which makes the long continuous brushstrokes difficult to complete. It was best to apply organic paint to a fully dried surface so it would be quickly absorbed and stick to itself where the lines joined. If there was any

Fig. 23. Crackling (crazing) in bottom of Mesa Verde Black-on-white bowl.

foreign matter on the surface, such as moisture or body oil from handling, the organic paint sometimes formed beads and was difficult to apply evenly.

Each modern potter has her own way of holding the pot and applying the paint. The left hand is often used inside the pot to hold it while the paint is being applied. Right-handed potters paint from left to right away from their bodies to prevent their hands from smearing the wet paint (Figure 11f). It is possible to determine the direction of most painted strokes on prehistoric pots by examining the ends of the stroke. Long, straight, fine lines were controlled by pressing nearly all of the long bristles of the yucca brush, not just the tip, against the surface.

Modern Pueblo potters do some planning before they apply the paint, but they do not use a pattern. This is the technique most probably used by Anasazi potters, who conceived their designs mentally and were remarkably skilled in adapting them to the shape of their vessels. Some modern Pueblo potters say they have no preconceived design; they allow the form of the vessel and the spirits in the clay to determine the design. A few prehistoric vessels show evidence of a false start and a design that was revised. On Mesa Verde over the centuries, the designs became increasingly standardized and more distinct from designs from other areas of the Anasazi world. The later Pueblo III painted wares have a relatively limited variety of layouts, designs, and elements and are distinct from any contemporary pottery of the Southwest. This seems to indicate an increase in the influence of cultural tradition on the potter's craft. Perhaps there was less contact with outside groups, and the aggregation of the inhabitants into fewer, larger communities during Pueblo III may have tended to standardize pottery-making practices through increased specialization of this craft. Fewer potters living closer together could have influenced the increased standardization in designs and forms in the Pueblo III pottery made on Mesa

Verde. It is interesting to note that some of the finest pottery made on Mesa Verde was created during the decades immediately prior to abandonment of this area in the late thirteenth century. Whatever the cause of this migration—and it would seem there would have been some social trauma—it did not adversely affect the work of these remarkable artisans.

Mineral paint does not adhere as well as organic paint, so the painter must be careful not to touch the painted surface while painting. After it dries, mineral paint is less sensitive to smearing. In order to improve adherence, prehistoric potters often mixed mineral paint with an organic medium. Thus, much of the paint used during the Pueblo II and III periods on Mesa Verde had both mineral and organic components, as did some pieces from the Pueblo I period. Flies were attracted to the sugar in carbon (organic) paint, and before it dried they may have eaten some of it, leaving thin spots in the design. Well-painted and well-fired Mesa Verde White Ware is nearly impervious to the elements in the dry climate of Mesa Verde. Some seven-hundred-year-old designs are nearly as bright as those on recently made Pueblo pottery.

Firing

The final crucial step in the pottery-making process was the firing. Mistakes made at this point might cause the pots to break, wasting all of the work done in the previous stages.

Prehistoric potters of the Southwest did not develop a true enclosed kiln. Their method of firing is known as nonkiln, clamp, or bonfire firing. The lack of an enclosed kiln limits the firing in several important aspects. The maximum temperature attainable in an open fire is limited. Studies indicate that the maximum temperature that can be reached in an open fire, with wood fuel, is approximately 962°C (Shepard, 1965). It is probable that the maximum temperatures attained in the bonfires of the Anasazi potters ranged from 600°C to 900°C. Thus, in modern terms, Anasazi pottery would be classified as terra cotta, which is fired below 1000°C. It has a high porosity and nowhere near the hardness of earthenwares, stonewares, or porcelain that require firing temperatures between 1000°C and 1400°C. The term "pottery" is more appropriate in referring to Anasazi ware than "ceramics," a term which describes high-fired, usually vitrified wares (Rice, 1987).

Almost as important as the maximum temperature attained in pottery firing, is the soaking time, or the time the pottery is subjected to the maximum heat. A bonfire reaches its maximum temperature quite rapidly, usually in ten to fifteen minutes, but the temperature soon begins to fall. It is not possible to maintain the maximum temperature for more than a few minutes. Also, the wind may cause the temperature to change quickly in part of the fire, causing uneven firing.

Another problem with open fires is that it is difficult to protect the pots from contact with the burning fuel, which causes carbon spots or fireclouds, or sometimes breaks the pot (Figure 24). It is a credit to the skill of the ancient potters that so few of the vessels they produced show any indication of incompetent firing. There were probably more "failures" than we are aware of, however, because we tend to find a larger proportion of the successes. As is evident from the description above, open firing is a risky process, and a number of vessels were probably lost during the firing process. (After stating the above, the writer recalled that during ten experimental firings at Mesa Verde in 1987-90, only three pieces, a solid figurine and two miniatures, were broken during firing. Perhaps we were just lucky, or perhaps when the cautions mentioned above are heeded the risk can be greatly reduced.)

Almost any fuel can be used to fire pottery. Today sheep and cow dung are the most common fuels used by the Pueblo potters. Of course, the Anasazi had no

Fig. 24. Chapin Gray vessels. *Upper:* Pitcher with firecloud from firing. *Lower row, left to right:* Seed jar; small bird jar; narrow necked, gourd-shaped jar.

combustible dung, so the fuel most likely used was wood. Utah Juniper (*Juniper utahensis*) was probably the preferred type of wood on Mesa Verde, because it is readily available and burns hotter and cleaner than other common indigenous woods. If juniper was not available, the potters on Mesa Verde could have used Piñon Pine, Douglas Fir, Gambel Oak, or a number of other species. The dry wood was cut or broken into pieces about one foot to one and a half feet long, and the larger pieces were split to produce fuel of the needed size. A large pottery firing requires quite a bit of fuel, so the collecting and preparation of the wood, with only stone tools, would require considerable effort. The fuel had to be dry so it would burn hot and not sputter or pop, which might have caused spots on the vessels. There are small outcroppings of coal on Mesa Verde, but there is no evidence that the Anasazi used it for pottery firing or heating.

Until recently no pottery firing pits had been found on Mesa Verde, but in late 1990 construction excavations on Chapin Mesa uncovered a shallow, 2.2 by 1.35 meter rock-lined pit (5MV3945) (Figure 50). The rock is smoke-blackened and the pit contained large amounts of wood ash and sherds from two Mancos Black-on-white bowls and a trough-shaped dipper, all of which appear to have been oxidized during one or more refirings. The characteristics of this pit, its contents, and its similarity to other pottery firing sites in the Northern San Juan area indicate it is probably a Pueblo II or III pottery firing site. One site on Wetherill Mesa, Site 1871, is listed as a possible corn roasting pit (Hayes, 1964), but it is possible that this was used for pottery firing.

A number of Pueblo III pottery firing pits have been found in the Yellow Jacket area northwest of Mesa Verde. These were located more than a mile from contemporary Anasazi dwellings (Fuller, 1984). A possible reason for this is that fuel was becoming scarce in the vicinity of the dwellings, and it was easier to carry the pots to the fuel than vice versa. It is possible that by the Pueblo III period, Mesa Verdeans were experiencing a serious shortage of fuel near their large habitation sites. Therefore, Pueblo III pottery firing pits on Mesa Verde may be some distance from the dwellings. Earlier, Basketmaker III and Pueblo I potters may have been able to fire their pots closer to their homes, because nearby fuel sources had not yet been depleted.

The firing areas in the Yellow Jacket area are roughly rectangular in shape and are partially or completely lined with stone slabs. They were excavated 20 to 40 centimeters below the surface, usually down to bedrock or gravelly deposits. They range from 1.85 to 5.2 meters in length and .9 to 2.0 meters in width. Sandstone cobbles, used to support the inverted vessels during firing, cover the floors of some areas. The Yellow Jacket firing sites contained Pueblo III white ware sherds, a few whole vessels of these types, and two

layers of wood ash (Fuller, 1984). The absence of Pueblo III gray ware sherds or vessels in these pits indicates white and gray wares may have been fired separately.

The ground area or shallow pit used for firing pottery must be dry, so the fire does not produce steam that will interfere with the firing. The Anasazi probably built a small fire on the site to dry out the ground. This fire would also be used for a final drying of the pots to be fired. Modern Pueblo potters employ this technique, sometimes called "water smoking." In order to get some of the fuel under the pots, it was necessary that the pots be supported by a low noncombustible platform. Thin sandstone slabs, cobbles, or large potsherds could have been used for this purpose. The pots to be fired were placed on this platform so the heat would surround them. Large numbers of pots were piled one on another in layers. Fuel was placed under the platform on the hot ground. The pots were protected from contact with the burning fuel by covering them carefully with large potsherds or thin sandstone slabs, if they were available. Pieces of wood fuel were then stacked around and on top of the pile of pots. If an oxidizing fire was desired, some openings were left in the fuel pile to permit the passage of oxygen through the fire. Morning hours were best for firings on Mesa Verde, because the wind was usually calm and there was less chance of rain.

The fire was probably lit in several places to produce even heating on all sides. Due to convection, the fuel under the pots provided much of the effective heat. Most of the heat from the fuel on top was lost through radiation and convection. Once the fire was burning well, there was little the potter could do to increase the heat. Adding more fuel did not significantly increase the heat reaching the pots.

Mesa Verde Black-on-white ware was fired in a partially oxidizing fire, as indicated by the black color of the carbon paint and the carbon streaks in the core of some of the sherds. If this clay was completely oxidized, the carbon paint would burn off and the clay would turn a brownish color. The partial oxidation was achieved by starting with an open oxidizing fire, then stopping the fire by covering it with sand or removing the pots before they became fully oxidized. If the fire was covered before the carbon in the fuel was consumed, the pots had to be removed before they were smudged black. Judging the right time to remove the pots took time and experience to learn. Several variables affected the degree of oxidation, and time was only one factor. Other variables included clay composition, method of fueling, and draft. Prehistoric potters probably used the color of the pots and appearance of the fire rather than the time to decide when to remove the pots and ensure a good black-on-white ware.

In some parts of the Southwest, the bonfire was purposely covered with finely ground fuel to produce a black carbon-covered surface on the vessel, but this was not done in the northern San Juan area. This smudging of the fire with finely ground dung was used by the famous potter Maria Martinez and other San Ildefonso and Santa Clara potters to produce the well-known modern matte-black-on-polished-black pottery.

Sticks were used to carefully remove the pots from the ashes. Closed forms, such as jars and pitchers, could be lifted out by inserting the end of the stick into them and gently removing them. Bowls were more difficult to remove and required steady handling with two sticks to lift them out. The pots were placed in a sheltered spot where they could cool, away from drafts, combustible material, and curious children. Once the pots had cooled they were wiped clean of ashes and possibly wiped with oil or washed. They were then ready for use.

The beautiful and utilitarian Anasazi pottery found in the ruins of Mesa Verde required much skill, experience, and patience to produce. The many important functions these prehistoric pottery vessels served are described in the next chapter.

FUNCTIONS OF PREHISTORIC POTTERY ON MESA VERDE

During the seven centuries of pottery production on Mesa Verde the unpainted gray wares were used primarily for the preparation and storage of food, and the decorated black-on-white and red wares for food service. Large narrow-necked ollas were made during all periods. These vessels had opposing loop handles low on the sides and were used as water containers (Figure 25). Some were used to carry water from seep springs to the dwellings or fields, but others, when filled with water, were too heavy for one person to carry over rough terrain. These very large ollas were probably used for short-term water storage. Perhaps each household had such a container in a room corner for family cooking and drinking water. Vessels with small mouths are better for transporting and storing water because they keep out foreign matter, decrease evaporation, and are less likely to spill.

Gray Ware

Early gray ware bowls were used for food preparation and food service. Wide-mouthed plain or corrugated jars were utilized for cooking; many show sooting from being used over a fire (Figure 26). Corrugated jars were also used for the storage of dry foods such as corn and beans. Thin, flat sandstone slabs have been found covering the mouths of these storage jars. Some of these lids were sealed with clay to keep out moisture, insects, and other pests. Small vessels with very small openings were uscd as canteens, with corn cob stoppers, to transport water on journeys through waterless areas. The wear patterns on dippers show they were used to dip water from pools at water sources, or to ladle food such as stew from a cooking jar into a serving bowl. They could also have been used as drinking vessels.

The reason for changing from entirely smoothed gray ware pots to the neckbanded types, such as Mancos Gray and Moccasin Gray, is not known. These types continued to be used for food preparation and storage, and the forms were restricted to wide-mouthed jars and pitchers. The great decrease in the variety of gray ware forms is related to the increase in decorated types which took over some of the functions previously served by undecorated gray wares. The new unobliterated neck coils may have made

Fig. 25. Moccasin Gray olla.

greasy cooking jars easier to hold than those with smooth necks. Another reason for this innovation may have been that the banded necks were more attractive to the Pueblo I and II era Anasazi.

Although several types of surface manipulations were produced in other parts of the world, corrugated vessels are unique to the prehistoric Southwest (Rice, 1987). Regular, well-formed corrugations produce an attractive vessel surface and the patterning of different types of corrugations and embellishments indicate that the Anasazi potters considered this a form of decoration. Corrugations also serve several utilitarian functions. In addition to providing a better grip on heavy jars, a rough surface improves the transfer of heat during cooking. A vessel with a corrugated surface has more surface area than a smooth vessel of the same shape and volume. Therefore, a corrugated ves-

sel both heats and cools more rapidly than a smooth one. The corrugations may also have made it easier to handle a hot vessel when it was removed by hand from a cooking fire. Another important use of large corrugated jars was long-term food storage. Particularly during Pueblo III times, they were commonly buried in the floors of rooms with the rim flush with the floor (Figure 27). Here they could be covered and used as safe storage places for all types of dry foodstuffs. Several of these storage jars have been found filled with kernels of corn. The sharply out-turned rims of the Mesa Verde Corrugated jars made them easier to lift and facilitated sealing them for storage. The manufacture of corru-

Fig. 26. Mesa Verde Corrugated jar on sandstone pot supports for use in cooking. Mug House, MVNP. (*Courtesy MVNP*)

42

gated vessels persisted for more than four hundred years on Mesa Verde, and even longer in other parts of the Southwest, indicating that this unique form of surface manipulation must have served a useful purpose for a long period of time.

Black-on-white Wares

Bowls were the most common black-on-white forms throughout the prehistoric era on Mesa Verde. The excavations during 1960-61 at Mug House, a Pueblo III cliff dwelling, produced 170 restorable black-on-white bowls and thousands of bowl sherds from other vessels. The larger decorated bowls were probably used to mix and serve food for a family, and the smaller ones were used to eat from. It is unlikely that each person had his or her own food bowl, because they probably sometimes ate directly from the cooking jar. Large globular ollas with short necks and opposing loop handles below the maximum diameter were used, as were

Fig. 27. Mesa Verde Corrugated storage jar buried in room floor. Long house, MVNP. (*Courtesy MVNP*)

the earlier plain gray ones, to transport and store water. Some of these ollas were decorated with corrugations around the neck (Figure 28).

Globular vessels with small openings in the top are called "seed jars." Their form makes them appropriate for holding small highly prized objects, such as the precious selected seeds carried over for planting the next year. Similarly shaped black-on-white jars with a low rim around the mouth and flat circular covers have been named "kiva jars" because they are found more frequently in kivas than in other rooms (Figures 29, 30, and 72).

The Anasazi in the northern San Juan area began to make unique black-on-white pottery mugs around A.D. 1000. Most of these vessels are very similar in shape to the modern beer mug. They are commonly in the shape of a truncated cone or less commonly cylindrical or globular. They have flat bottoms and a flat or round handle extending from just below the rim to near the base (Figures 19 and 31). It appears that these mugs were drinking vessels used to drink water and other liquids such as soup. The globular "mugs" with sharply out-turned rims are not well suited to drinking and were probably small pitchers. A few double mugs joined by a solid handle at the rim and a hollow tube near the base have been found on Mesa Verde and at other sites in the area (Figure 32) (Oppelt, 1989). As Mesa Verde-style mugs increased in popularity, pitcher forms decreased, indicating that mugs had taken over some of the functions of pitchers. After the abandonment of the Four Corners region in the late thirteenth century, some of the migrant Anasazi continued to make Mesa Verde White Ware in the common forms, except for mugs and kiva jars which were no longer produced.

During the later periods of the prehistoric habitation of Mesa Verde, a few pottery smoking pipes were produced. A small cache of these was found at Pipe Shrine House in Far View Community on Chapin Mesa

Top left:
Fig. 28. Mesa Verde Black-on-white jar with corrugated neck and pair of mending holes.

Bottom:
Fig. 29. Mesa Verde Black-on-white kiva jar with overall design and pairs of holes for securing lid.

Top right:
Fig. 30. Mesa Verde Black-on-white kiva jar with banded design.

Fig. 31. Mesa Verde Black-on-white mugs with banded designs.

Fig. 32. Mesa Verde Black-on-white double mug from Mug House. MVNP. (*Courtesy MVNP*)

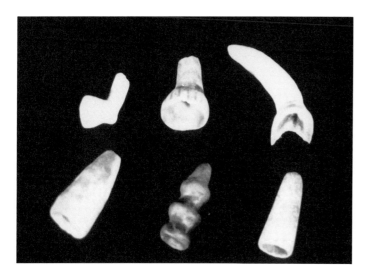

Fig. 33. Clay pipes from Basketmaker III and Pueblo I periods. Badger House Community, MVNP.

Fig. 34. Burials with pottery and other grave goods. Pithouse, Site 1676, Badger House Community, MVNP. (*Courtesy MVNP*)

(Fewkes, 1923). The small number of pipes recovered on Mesa Verde indicates that smoking was probably done only in ceremonies or by a few individuals (Figure 33).

A variety of other black-on-white pottery forms were made on Mesa Verde, particularly during the Basketmaker III and Pueblo I periods. These include double-spouted vessels, platters, gourd-shaped jars, half-gourd ladles, and a variety of miniature vessels. Except for a few early jars which are roughly bird shaped, effigy vessels are very rare on Mesa Verde. Beyond Mesa Verde, effigies are more common and of better quality in Cortez Black-on-white and Mancos Black-on-white than the later types.

The Anasazi commonly placed pottery in burials with the remains of their deceased. The presence of pottery and other artifacts in many burials indicates that the Anasazi may have believed in some type of journey after death, or in an afterlife. Bowls are the most common form of pottery found in graves, but mugs, pitchers, jars, and dippers have also been discovered (Figure 34). Some grave bowls contain organic residues indicating they may have contained food for the deceased's afterlife. The bowls in the graves at Mug House exhibit a larger proportion of mending than those from other locations in the ruin. Mended bowls may have been considered preferable for use in the life after death. Small corrugated jars were also placed with human remains; some contained small artifacts such as craftsman's tools or items of personal adornment. Other articles commonly found as grave goods are stone tools, bone awls, sandals, jewelry, and mats. The amount and rarity of grave goods in a community's burials give some indication of its wealth. High-status burials with many or unusual grave goods are unknown on Mesa Verde.

After a pot was broken, the pieces, known as potsherds or sherds, were utilized in a number of ways. As previously noted, in the later time periods, potsherds were ground and used as temper in pottery clay. Thus, pots were made from the remains of their predecessors and some particles of temper were used in several generations of pots. Potsherds were used in several other ways in the production of pottery. Large shallow sherds with smoothed edges were used as pot rests to support rounded vessel bases during formation and to cover pots during the firing process. The designs on old potsherds may have been used by Anasazi potters as patterns for their painted designs. This practice has been common with historic Pueblo potters, notably the Hopi/Tewa potter Nampeyo, who initiated the revival of pottery making on First Mesa in the late nineteenth century.

The Mesa Verdeans prized their pottery because of the great skill and effort that went into its production. When a pot developed a crack, it was carefully mended to prevent further damage. The usual method of mend-

Fig. 35. Yucca twine mend on exterior of Mesa Verde Black-on-white bowl. Mug House, MVNP. (*Courtesy MVNP*)

ing painted pieces was to drill one or more pairs of small opposing holes on either side of the crack. Twine made of yucca fibers was threaded through each pair of holes and tightly tied to pull the sides of the crack together (Figures 22 and 35). Bowls were more often mended than were jars, mugs, or dippers. Because corrugated utility jars were often placed over cooking fires, the use of twine as described above was not feasible. Corrugated vessels were mended by melting pine pitch and spreading it over the crack on the interior of the jar. The fact that black-on-white serving vessels were more commonly mended than plain or corrugated utility pots may indicate that the former were more highly valued, or that it was difficult to effectively repair a vessel used for either food storage or preparation.

Pottery sherds were modified or "worked" into a variety of useful objects including pottery scrapers, spindle whorls, pendants, scoops, jar covers, knives, and gaming pieces. Decorated sherds were used in preference to plain or corrugated ones. During the Anasazi

tenure on Mesa Verde, there was an increase in the production of modified sherds and in the uses of broken pottery (Oppelt, 1984) (Figure 36).

Potsherds were also used as chinking stones in the mortar of masonry walls. These small pieces served to lessen the effects of drying and cracking in wide courses of mortar. The short necks of Pueblo III black-on-white ollas were used to line the interior of some kiva sipapus. Several of these are visible at Long House and Mug House on Wetherill Mesa (Figure 37).

Red Ware

The small amount of restorable red ware pottery found on Mesa Verde makes it impossible to determine much about its functions. From the limited data and information gathered at sites outside Mesa Verde, it appears that red wares and black-on-white wares were used in similar ways, primarily for food service and storage of small objects.

Fig. 36. Worked potsherds, Mancos Black-on-white and Mesa Verde Black-on-white.

Fig. 37. Mesa Verde White Ware jar neck lining sipapu in kiva floor. Mug House, MVNP.

THE DEVELOPMENT OF
POTTERY ON MESA VERDE

The following chapter presents a synthesis of the development of prehistoric pottery over seven centuries on Mesa Verde. This development is similar to that in the rest of the northern San Juan, but differs in some important aspects. Mesa Verde was not the center of population in the northern San Juan area during the Basketmaker III to Pueblo III times, and was not necessarily typical of the surrounding area. The eight very large villages in the Montezuma Valley near Cortez, Colorado, comprised the densest population center during Pueblo III times. Current excavation in several of these large villages, especially Sand Canyon and Yellow Jacket, may answer some questions about the prehistoric pottery of this area.

The approximate periods of production of the pottery types described in this chapter are shown in Table 2.

The Gray Ware Tradition

The earliest pottery found on Mesa Verde is a plain gray type known as Chapin Gray (Morris, 1939). Its beginnings coincide roughly with the movement of the first Anasazi onto Mesa Verde. The manufacture of this first gray ware was developing during the immigration of the Basketmakers from sites in the valleys to the north, circa A.D. 575 to 600. As the Basketmakers improved their cultivation of corn, beans, and squash and became more sedentary, pottery became increasingly useful. This first pottery was well constructed with thin, hard walls, indicating that the technique was probably adopted from another area rather than a local invention (Figures 38 and 39). This pottery was made by coiling and scraping as described in Chapter Three. The coils were usually smoothed but rarely polished. The surface on most Chapin Gray vessels has a gritty feel, which is caused by temper particles that protruded when the vessel surface was scraped while it was "leather" hard (Figure 40). This type was tempered with crushed igneous rock and occasionally some crushed sandstone, and was fired in a partially oxidizing atmosphere. Chapin Gray was made in a variety of shapes, with jars predominating (Figure 24). Some Chapin Gray vessels have shapes mimicking gourd vessels that were used before the advent of pottery (Figure 24).

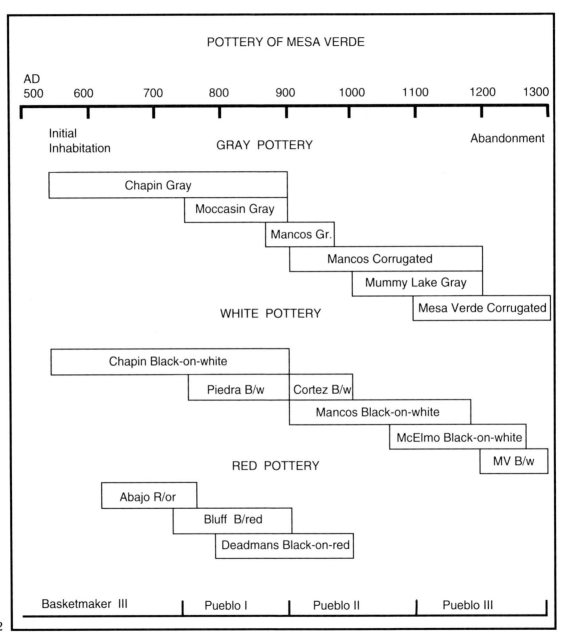

POTTERY OF MESA VERDE

AD
500   600   700   800   900   1000   1100   1200   1300

Initial
Inhabitation   GRAY POTTERY   Abandonment

Chapin Gray

Moccasin Gray

Mancos Gr.

Mancos Corrugated

Mummy Lake Gray

Mesa Verde Corrugated

WHITE POTTERY

Chapin Black-on-white

Piedra B/w   Cortez B/w

Mancos Black-on-white

McElmo Black-on-white

MV B/w

RED POTTERY

Abajo R/or

Bluff B/red

Deadmans Black-on-red

Basketmaker III   Pueblo I   Pueblo II   Pueblo III

Table 2

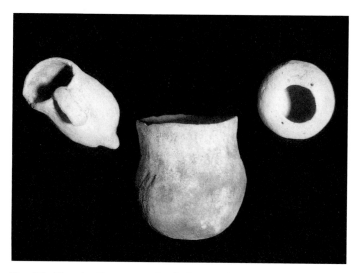

Fig. 38. Chapin Gray vessels. *Left to right*: Miniature bird jar, small wide-mouthed jar, and miniature seed jar.

Fig. 39. Chapin Gray olla.

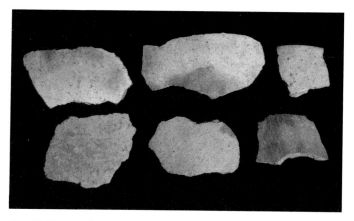

Fig. 40. Chapin Gray sherds, showing rough surface and protruding temper particles.

On Mesa Verde, this early pottery is known from surface collections and a number of excavated mesa-top pithouses. A few pithouses have also been found in cliff alcoves, notably those in the south end of Step House cave; these have been excavated and restored for interpretation. The Chapin Grey type sites on Mesa Verde are located on Ruins Road on Chapin Mesa and include Deep Pithouse, Site 101; Pithouse B, Site 117; and Site 145. Other type sites include Badger House Community and Step House on Wetherill Mesa (Map 4). Chapin Gray is less common than most later types because the population was smaller in the earlier years, the pithouses were well covered by centuries of wind-blown soil, and the villages lacked the large trash mounds of the later aggregated sites.

A variety of Chapin Gray, known as Fugitive Red, had an impermanent red ochre wash applied to the surface after firing (Plate 3). A polished variety has been named Twin Trees Plain by Deric O'Bryan (1950), but it has not been accepted as a valid type by most researchers. Chapin Gray is identical to other Basketmaker types, such as Lino Gray and Obelisk Gray, from other areas of the Anasazi region, although the latter two have sand temper and Obelisk Gray has a polished surface.

Chapin Gray represents the beginning of the long gray ware tradition on Mesa Verde. Chapin Gray, as a type, was made from A.D. 575 to 900, and Mesa Verde Gray Ware continued in several other types for four centuries until the abandonment of Mesa Verde in the late thirteenth century. Its range was the northern drainage of the San Juan River from the La Plata River Valley west to the Abajo Mountains in southeastern Utah (Map 3).

The second development in the Mesa Verde Gray Ware tradition that has been classified as a type is the appearance of wide unobliterated coils on the necks of jars, ollas, and pitchers. This Pueblo I type, made from A.D. 775 to 900, has been given the name Moccasin Gray (Morris, 1939; Rohn, 1977) (Figures 41 and 42). Moccasin Gray type sites include sites 103, 111, and 786 on Chapin Mesa, and Badger House Community on Wetherill Mesa (Map 4). Body sherds of Moccasin Gray cannot be distinguished from those of Chapin Gray. As in Chapin Gray, the temper in Moccasin Gray is predominantly crushed igneous rock. Some Chapin Gray vessels have loop or lug handles and the vessel rims are usually tapered or less commonly are rounded.

Another similar gray ware type, Mancos Gray (Rohn, 1977), was made during the transition between the Pueblo I and Pueblo II periods, circa A.D. 875 to 950. It differs from Moccasin Gray in having narrower unobliterated neck coils with more overlap. Some vessels of this type are grooved with a pointed tool between the coils (Figures 15 and 43). In other parts of the Southwest, overlapping coils are sometimes referred to as clapboard corrugated. The common shapes continue as necked jars, cauldron-shaped jars, and pitchers. All other characteristics of construction are the same as Chapin Gray and Moccasin Gray. It should be noted that the smoothed gray ware types were formed with concentric coils, but the later corrugated types were

Fig. 41. Moccasin Gray jar, showing wide, unobliterated coils on neck.

Fig. 42. Moccasin Gray pitcher, showing unobliterated coils on neck and handle of two unsmoothed coils.

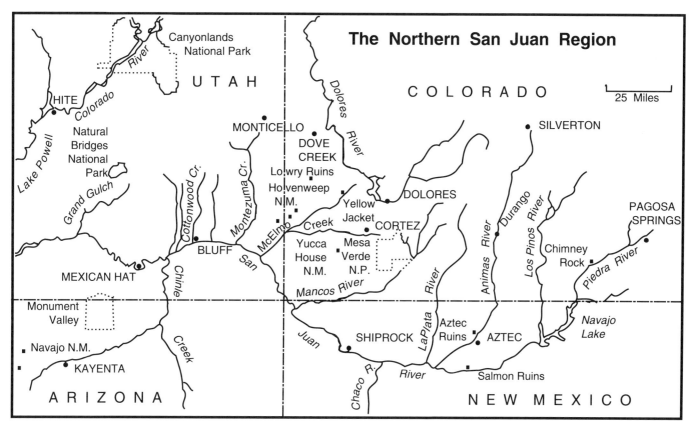

The Northern San Juan Region

Map 3

coiled in a spiral manner. The type site for Mancos Gray is Site 16 on Chapin Mesa near Twin Trees (Map 4).

Another very rare gray utility type, Mummy Lake Gray (Rohn and Swannack, 1965), made during Pueblo II and early Pueblo III times (A.D. 950 to 1200), is similar to the two preceding types in most attributes. It differs only in having a single flat coil of clay added to the finished rim, which is erected from the wall (Figure 16). The remainder of the surface is smoothed as in Chapin Gray. The common shapes of vessels of this type are similar to the later corrugated types, such as wide-mouthed jars and pitchers (Figures 44 and 45). The type sites for Mummy Lake Gray are Site 875 on Chapin Mesa, and Badger House, Big Juniper House, and Two Raven House on Wetherill Mesa.

The first corrugated type made on Mesa Verde is known as Mancos Corrugated (Rohn, 1977). Its basic construction methods are similar to the earlier gray ware types, but it differs in surface manipulation and rim shape. The surface of the vessel is covered with corrugations formed by pinching the soft coils with a finger or pressing with a tool. The rims are similar to

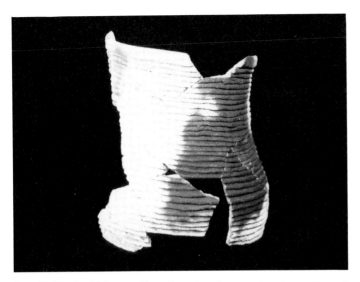

Fig. 43. Neck of Mancos Gray jar, showing overlapping coils and large fire cloud.

Fig. 45. Mummy Lake Gray pitcher with single fillet below rim.

Fig. 44. Mummy Lake Gray jar with single fillet below the rim.

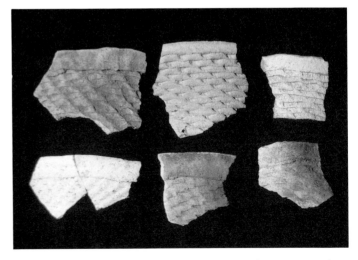

Fig. 46. Mancos Corrugated rim sherds, note direct rims in line with neck.

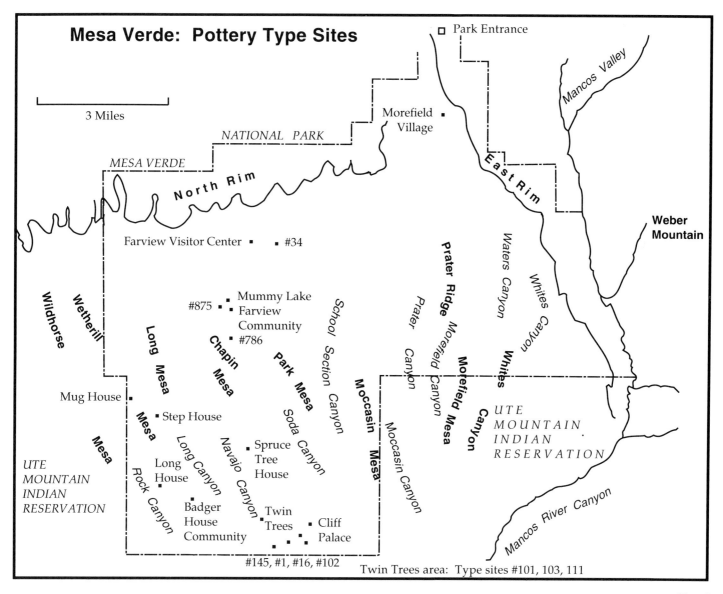

Mesa Verde: Pottery Type Sites

□ Park Entrance

3 Miles

MESA VERDE NATIONAL PARK

Mancos Valley

North Rim

East Rim

Morefield Village

Weber Mountain

Farview Visitor Center ■ ■ #34

Wildhorse

Wetherill

#875 ■ ■ Mummy Lake
Farview
Community
■ #786

Long Mesa

Chapin Mesa

Park Mesa

School Section Canyon

Moccasin Mesa

Prater Ridge

Waters Canyon

Whites Canyon

Prater Canyon

Morefield Canyon

Morefield Mesa

Whites Canyon

Mug House ■

Mesa

Step House ■

Long Canyon

Navajo Canyon

Soda Canyon

Moccasin Canyon

UTE MOUNTAIN INDIAN RESERVATION

Mesa

Rock Canyon

Long House ■

Spruce Tree House ■

Badger House Community

Twin Trees ■

Cliff Palace ■

UTE MOUNTAIN INDIAN RESERVATION

Mancos River Canyon

#145, #1, #16, #102

Twin Trees area: Type sites #101, 103, 111

Map 4

Mummy Lake Gray except that they were continued directly from the walls rather than turned out from the body (Figure 46). The shapes are predominantly wide-mouthed jars with a few pitchers and necked jars (Figure 47). The term usually used to describe the jars is "cauldron shaped." The type is usually unpainted, but a few jars have simple markings on the rim interiors and very rarely some paint on the corrugated exterior (Figure 48). Mancos Corrugated is a Pueblo II and early Pueblo III type, made between A.D. 900 and 1200. The type site on Mesa Verde is Site 16 on Chapin Mesa (Map 4).

A later type very similar to Mancos Corrugated is known as Mesa Verde Corrugated (Morris, 1939; Rohn, 1977). The body sherds from these two types are nearly identical. They differ only in the shape of their rims and to a lesser degree in vessel body shapes. Mesa Verde Corrugated has sharply out-turned rims in contrast to the Mancos Corrugated rims that continue directly from the wall (Figure 49). Mesa Verde Corrugated jars have an egg shape, with the largest diameter near the base, whereas Mancos Corrugated jars are more cylindrical (Figures 51 and 52). Mesa Verde Corrugated was made from A.D. 1100 to the abandonment of Mesa Verde, circa A.D. 1300. This type is very common in Pueblo III cliff dwellings. The basic construction is the same as the earlier gray ware types with crushed igneous rock used as the primary temper material. The corrugations are the same as Mancos Corrugated, although they seem to be finer and more even on many vessels. Deviations from this type include patterns formed of areas of plain coils among the indented coils (Figure 17). There are also a few vessels of this type with corrugations to the rim, small applique designs near the rim, or bottoms smoothed rather than corrugated (Figures 51 and 53).

The type sites for Mesa Verde Corrugated are the well-known Pueblo III cliff dwellings of Cliff Palace and Spruce Tree House, and Mug House on Wetherill Mesa

Fig. 47. Mancos Corrugated jar and pitcher showing direct rims.

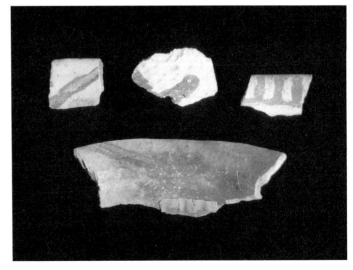

Fig. 48. Painted designs on interior rims of corrugated jars. *Upper center*: Painted design on exterior of a corrugated vessel.

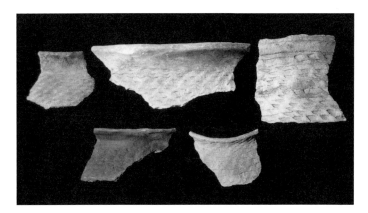

Fig. 49. Mesa Verde Corrugated rim sherds showing out turned (everted) rims.

Fig. 50. Pueblo II firing pit (5MV 3945), Chapin Mesa, MVNP. (*Courtesy MVNP*)

Fig. 51. Mesa Verde Corrugated coil jar with applique decoration.

Fig. 52. Small Mesa Verde Corrugated jar and pitcher.

(Map 4). The gray ware tradition persisted on Mesa Verde for seven hundred years with only the attributes of surface manipulation, and rim and body shape varying significantly. Although the temper in Mesa Verde White Ware changed over the centuries from predominantly crushed igneous rock to crushed pot sherds, the Mesa Verde Gray Utility Ware was tempered with large proportions of igneous rock during the entire period of its production. The reason for this may be that the large proportion of igneous particles protected the pots from thermal shock when they were used for cooking food. Mancos Corrugated and Mesa Verde Corrugated were produced in the northern drainages of the San Juan River from the Animas River west to the Colorado River.

Hovenweep Corrugated (Hayes, 1964) is a sand-tempered variation of Mesa Verde Corrugated. It has more deeply indented corrugations extending to the rim, and the jars are globular in shape when compared with the egg-shaped Mesa Verde Corrugated jars. This type has been identified from the Anasazi ruins in Hovenweep National Monument to the west of Mesa Verde, along the Colorado-Utah border (Hayes, 1964).

White Ware Tradition

The second pottery tradition on Mesa Verde is the well-known painted white ware. This tradition lasted from A.D. 575 to the abandonment, circa A.D. 1300. As was the gray ware, this ware was constructed by the coil-and-scrape method. The earlier types are unslipped and have a somewhat rough exterior similar to Chapin Gray. The later types are smoothed or polished and usually white slipped. A few white ware vessels have corrugations on the exteriors of bowls or on the necks of short-necked ollas (Figures 54, 55, and 56). The black designs on this ware were painted in mineral and/or carbon pigments and fired in a reducing-to-oxidizing atmosphere.

Fig. 53. Smoothed base on Mesa Verde Corrugated jar.

Chapin Black-on-white, made and used on Mesa Verde between A.D. 575 and 900, was the first painted type (Abel, 1955; Rohn, 1977). It decreased after A.D. 750 and was replaced by the neckbanded types. Chapin Black-on-white is unslipped and is basically Chapin Gray with black painted designs. The paint is predominantly mineral with carbon on a few vessels. The designs are isolated with the majority of the surface unpainted. The lines are usually poorly drawn and radiate from the center or are organized in straight or zigzag panels (Figures 57, 58, 59, 60, and Plate 6). Small circles are common in the centers of bowls. Dots, stepped elements, crosses, and dashes are frequently used as fillers between parallel lines. The concentric layouts so common in later types are rare in Chapin Black-on-white. Some of the designs and elements are

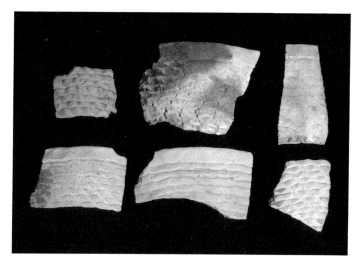

Fig. 54. Mancos Black-on-white bowl sherds showing corrugated exteriors.

Fig. 55. Mancos Black-on-white bowl with corrugated exterior.

Fig. 56. Corrugated exterior of Mancos Black-on-white bowl shown in Fig. 55. (Unusual painted circle on base.)

Fig. 57. Chapin Black-on-white sherds showing representative designs. Step House pithouses, MVNP. (*Courtesy MVNP*)

Fig. 58. Chapin Black-on-white sherds with representative designs. Upper center shows "z"s typical of basket designs.

Fig. 59. Chapin Black-on-white bowls.

similar to those on basketry with designs built up from the bottom. One design, the "basket stitch," is particularly reminiscent of the short "z"s on Basketmaker baskets (Figure 58). The paint color ranges from black to reddish-brown. The latter color results from oxidation of the mineral paint containing iron. The most common shape is the hemispherical bowl, although long-necked ollas, pitchers, seed jars, and half-gourd ladles have also been found.

The range of this type extends north of the San Juan River from the Animas River west to the Colorado River in Utah. The type sites on Chapin Mesa are excavated pithouses: Site 101; Pithouse B, Site 117; Pithouse A, Site 118; and Site 145 (Map 4). Chapin Black-on-white was formerly called La Plata Black-on-white, which differs in that it was sandtempered. The name Lino Black-on-white refers to a similar sand-tempered type made south of the San Juan River.

Piedra Black-on-white (Hayes, 1964; Rohn, 1977), a Pueblo I type, was made circa A.D. 750 to 900. It differs from Chapin Black-on-white chiefly in the characteristics of its design elements and the method used to produce them. Chapin Black-on-white designs are made with shorter strokes and are more like the designs on basketry. Unattached elements are common in Piedra Black-on-white vessels. Lines are commonly elaborated with slashes, short lines, or dots. A squiggle line is sometimes superimposed over a straight line. Two or more parallel lines are common (Figures 1a, 1b, and 61). Band layouts, so common in later types, are rare in Piedra Black-on-white pots. Vessels of this type have smoother surfaces than Chapin Black-on-white Ware, and 10 percent of the sherds of this type from Mesa Verde are white slipped. The paint on Piedra Black-on-white vessels is mainly mineral with 5 percent of the sherds having carbon paint. Bowls are the most common form in this type; other common shapes are jars, gourd-shaped jars, seed jars, and ladles (Figures 1a and 1b).

Fig. 60. Large Chapin Black-on-white seed jar with simple band.

The range of Piedra Black-on-white is more restricted than the other Mesa Verde painted types. It is found only in the northern drainage of the San Juan River from the Piedra River to the Mancos River drainage. It has not been found in southeastern Utah. This type is found in Mesa Verde National Park at type Sites 103 and 786, both on Chapin Mesa (Map 4). Piedra Black-on-white is uncommon compared to other black-on-white types on Mesa Verde. It is found primarily in the Pueblo I mesa-top villages, few of which have been excavated.

A type common in the Pueblo II sites on Mesa Verde has been named Cortez Black-on-white (Rohn, 1977; Swannack, 1969). It was made circa A.D. 900 to 1000. Cortez Black-on-white was produced after A.D. 1000 in decreasing amounts through the Pueblo II period, and has been used by archaeologists as a horizon marker for the Pueblo II period. The common forms of this type

are bowls, pitchers, narrow-necked jars, seed jars, and eccentric forms (Figure 62). The seed jars are more globular than in previous types and some jars have indented bases. Many vessels have polished surfaces and nearly all are white slipped. The paint on this type is mainly mineral in a well-controlled organic (carbon) medium. The most common elements in the painted designs are parallel lines, scrolls, and ticked triangles (triangles bordered with small dots or lines). Straight-line and squiggle-line hatching are introduced in this type (Figures 63 and 64). More of the design layouts are banded and some are indistinguishable from those appearing later on Mancos Black-on-white ware. A few Cortez Black-on-white bowls have corrugated exteriors. The designs used on this ware are similar to those on Kiatuthlanna Black-on-white and Red Mesa Black-on-white made to the south in northwestern New Mexico during the same time. Although Cortez Black-on-white is a distinctive, well-made pottery type, it is likely that the vessel forms and technology were influenced by styles from the southern parts of the Anasazi region.

Fig. 61. Piedra Black-on-white sherds with representative designs.

Fig. 62. Cortez Black-on-white bowl and pitcher with typical design layouts and elements.

The Mesa Verde type sites for Cortez Black-on-white are Site 16 on Chapin Mesa, and Site 1452, Badger House Community, on Wetherill Mesa (Map 4). Cortez Black-on-white is distributed from the area around Durango, Colorado, west to the Abajo Mountains in Utah, and north from the San Juan River to the Dolores River and Dove Creek, Colorado.

Mancos Black-on-white (Martin, 1936; Rohn, 1977) is a very common type in the Pueblo II sites on Mesa Verde. It was made during the entire Pueblo II period and into early Pueblo III times, A.D. 900 to 1150. It is characterized by a great variety of painted designs. Layouts include broad bands, overall patterns and less commonly, segmented layouts. The band layouts do not have parallel framer lines bordering the band. The common design elements on Mancos Black-on-white include triangles in a variety of shapes, hatching, checkerboards, squiggle lines, parallel lines, dots, and

broadline frets (Figure 65). Rims are usually tapered and rounded on the lip; they may be plain, solidly painted, or less commonly ticked.

Mancos Black-on-white occurs from the Piedra River area west to the Abajo Mountains in southeastern Utah and from the San Juan River north to the Dolores River. The type sites on Mesa Verde are Site 16 on Chapin Mesa and Big Juniper House on Wetherill Mesa (Map 4). A number of vessels of this type have flat strap-shaped handles. Vessel shapes are similar to those of Cortez Black-on-white, except there are fewer pitchers and squash pots (Figures 66, 67, and 68). Half-gourd and strap-handle dippers are less common and tubular-handled dippers appear. Vessel walls are somewhat thicker than in Cortez Black-on-white. The Mesa Verde-style mug was introduced during this era in sites northwest of Mesa Verde, but it has not been found among pottery of this type on Mesa Verde. Two devia-

Plate 7
Black-on-white bowls.

Plate 8
Abajo Red-on-orange pitcher.

Plate 9
Abajo Red-on-orange seed jar.

Plate 10
San Juan Red ware sherds. *Upper row*: Abajo Red-on-orange. *Middle row*: Bluff Black-on-red. *Lower row*: Deadmans Black-on-red.

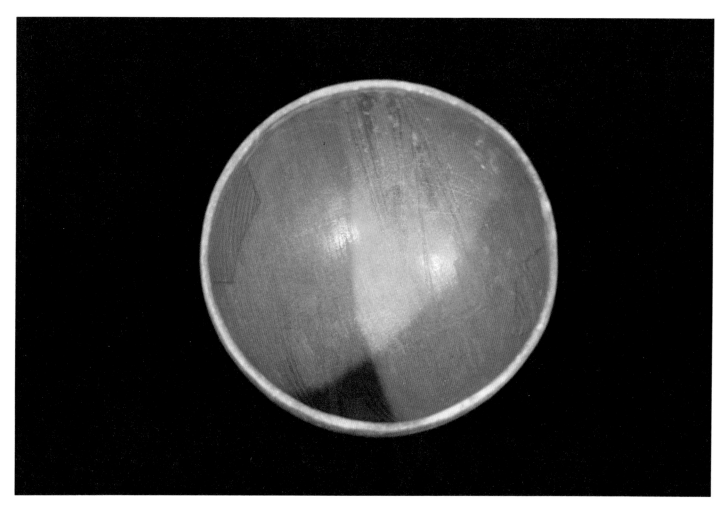

Plate 11
Deadmans Black-on-red bowl.

Plate 12
Common intrusive pottery types on Mesa Verde. *Upper row*: Red Mesa Black-on-white, Escavada Black-on-white, and Gallup Black-on-white. *Second row*: Wingate Black-on-red. *Third row*: Puerco Black-on-red and Wingate (Houck) Polychrome. *Bottom row*: Tusayan Black-on-red and Tusayan Polychrome.

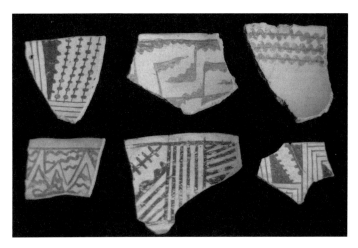

Fig. 63. Cortez Black-on-white rim sherds with representative designs.

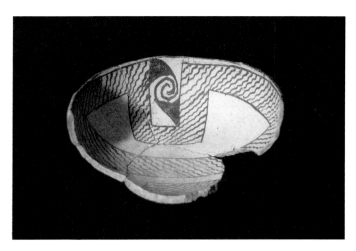

Fig. 64. Partial Cortez Black-on-white bowl with squiggle hatching and interlocking scroll designs.

tions of this type have been named: Morefield Black-on-gray (Abel, 1955), an unslipped variety; and Wetherill Black-on-white (Hayes, 1964), which are vessels with organic paint. Neither of these variations has gained general acceptance as a separate type. Corrugated exteriors are most common in bowls of this type, making up 5 percent of all vessels of this form (Figure 55).

McElmo Black-on-white (Hayes, 1964; Rohn, 1971) is a late Pueblo II through Pueblo III type made from A.D. 1075 to 1275. Some researchers view it as a variety of Mesa Verde Black-on-white rather than a separate type. The criteria for separating McElmo Black-on-white from Mesa Verde Black-on-white are somewhat subjective. Therefore, many sherds cannot be classified. Throughout the entire range of McElmo Black-on-white the material used as temper varies, but on Mesa Verde, 75 percent of the sherds of this type have crushed potsherd temper. The remainder were tempered with crushed igneous rock. Common shapes in this type are bowls, narrow-necked ollas, seed jars, pitchers, and mugs (Figure 69).

Most of the paint on McElmo Black-on-white found on Mesa Verde has organic pigment. Painted designs show continual change, from the earliest, which are similar to Mancos Black-on-white, to the later vessels, with designs almost identical to Mesa Verde Black-on-white (Figure 70). Some designs are poorly executed Mesa Verde Black-on-white ones. Other designs are well-done combinations of Mancos Black-on-white elements, although triangles are less common than on Mesa Verde Black-on-white. Heavy solid lines are common and may be opposed by similar elements of fine parallel lines. The surfaces of McElmo Black-on-white vessels are usually smoothed and may be polished over the painted designs. The Mesa Verde type sites for McElmo Black-on-white are Cliff Palace, Spruce Tree House, and Mug House (Map 4).

The final painted white ware made on Mesa Verde is the classic Pueblo III Mesa Verde Black-on-white (Morris, 1939; Rohn, 1971). It was made from A.D. 1200 to abandonment, circa A.D. 1300. Its major attributes are almost identical to McElmo Black-on-white. The slip is

Fig. 65. Mancos Black-on-white rim sherds with typical designs in mineral or carbon paint.

Fig. 66. Large Mancos Black-on-white bowl, mug, and dipper.

Fig. 67. Mancos Black-on-white dipper bowls and a small narrow-mouthed jar.

Fig. 68. Black-on-white bowls. *Left*: Mineral paint. *Right*: Carbon paint.

Fig. 69. McElmo Black-on-white bowl and small mug with key-hole cutout in handle.

Fig. 70. McElmo Black-on-white rim sherds with representative designs.

an even white or pearl gray that is sometimes thick and crackled. Bowls continue as the most common form, and mugs and kiva jars are more common than in Mc-Elmo Black-on-white (Figures 28, 29, 30, 31, 71, and 72).

On Mesa Verde, the paint on this type is mainly organic, but to the west, mineral paint was more common. A variant with both mineral and organic paint has been named Mesa Verde Polychrome (Abel, 1955) (Figure 3). Bowl exteriors are more frequently decorated than in earlier types. On all forms, the most common design layout is a band divided into smaller and smaller segments (Figure 73). A few vessels have centered or offset overall layouts (Figures 74 and 75). The layouts are nearly always symmetrical or balanced. The banded layouts are frequently bordered by narrow and/or wide framing lines. Hatching is used as a background filler particularly in the overall and offset layouts, and dots are used between parallel lines and on the edges of solid elements. Anthropomorphic and zoomorphic figures are rare, but they sometimes ap-

pear as isolated figures in the center of bowl interiors or on exterior bowl walls (Figures 76 and 77). Common elements in Mesa Verde Black-on-white designs are opposing stepped triangles, opposing ticked triangles, checkerboards, interlocking scrolls, frets, chevrons or zigzag lines, and parallel lines in a great variety of patterns. The brushwork in the painted designs of this type is nearly always well executed. Vessel rims are commonly flattened, and almost all are ticked with small elements such as dots, lines, bars, or zigzags (Figure 78).

Mesa Verde Black-on-white ranges from the Durango area west to the Colorado River and north to the Dolores River, but it also occurs to the south in Chaco Canyon and up Chinle Wash to Canyon de Chelly in northeastern Arizona. The type sites are the same as those for McElmo Black-on-white. Mesa Verde Black-on-white is the classic painted pottery associated with the well-known Pueblo III cliff dwellings of Mesa Verde National Park.

Top:
Fig. 71. Mesa Verde Black-on-white jar with banded design and pierced lug handles.

Bottom left:
Fig. 72. Large Mesa Verde Black-on-white kiva jar. (*Courtesy MVNP*)

Bottom right:
Fig. 73. Mesa Verde Black-on-white partial bowl with band design layout and enigmatic central figure.

Top left:
Fig. 74. Mesa Verde Black-on-white bowl with over-all, centered four part design layout.

Top right:
Fig. 75. Mesa Verde Black-on-white bowl with over-all design. Long House, MVNP. (*Courtesy MVNP*)

Bottom:
Fig. 76. Mesa Verde Black-on-white bowl, portion of bottom with four human figures. Long House, MVNP. (*Courtesy MVNP*)

Fig. 77. Mesa Verde or McElmo Black-on-white dipper, portion with figure of horned toad in bottom. Long House, MVNP (*Courtesy of MVNP.*)

In summary, the white ware tradition on Mesa Verde lasted for seven hundred years during which the basic technology of manufacture remained the same, but the following changes occurred (Plate 7):

1. Earlier types were made in a variety of forms, but by Pueblo III times the forms became more standardized. There was also a shift from gourd-portion forms in the earlier types to independent shapes that did not copy any earlier containers.

2. The predominant temper material changed from crushed igneous rock to crushed potsherds.

3. The most commonly used paint changed from mineral pigment to organic (carbon) paint.

4. The average thickness of vessel walls increased.

5. The common rim shape changed from tapered to rounded and then to flattened, and from plain or solidly painted to nearly all ticked.

6. The finishing of vessel surfaces changed from unslipped to slipped and from poorly smoothed to well-smoothed or polished.

7. The percentage of corrugated exteriors on white ware bowls increased to a peak represented by Mancos Black-on-white (A.D. 900 to 1150), then decreased.

8. The variety of motifs in the painted designs increased from Chapin Black-on-white to Mancos Black-on-white, then decreased through Mesa Verde Black-on-white.

The reasons for most of the above changes are unknown. There may have been influences from other areas or from immigrants, or perhaps changes in the preferences of local potters over time. The designs on Mesa Verde White Ware are more similar to those of other Anasazi branches in Basketmaker III and Pueblo II periods than they are in Pueblo I and Pueblo III times. The classic Mesa Verde Black-on-white made during the century prior to abandonment is easily distin-

Fig. 78. Mesa Verde Black-on-white bowl, jar, and mug sherds with representative designs in carbon paint.

guished from any other prehistoric pottery of the Southwest, although Galisteo Black-on-white made later in the area south of Santa Fe is quite similar.

Red Ware Tradition

The third pottery tradition on Mesa Verde is the distinctive San Juan Red Ware. Its approximate dates of manufacture are A.D. 700 to 1000, and it was most common during Pueblo I times. This ware required a different firing technique from that of the gray and white wares. In order to produce the red ware, it was necessary to fire in an oxidizing atmosphere with free oxygen or in a neutral atmosphere. This caused the iron in the clay to oxidize and turn red. The clay used was different from that in the white ware, and its source on Mesa Verde has not been located. There are several unanswered questions concerning this red ware.

The earliest Mesa Verde red ware type is known as Abajo Red-on-orange (Brew, 1946). This type is usually unslipped with a surface color of orange to red decorated with a reddish black paint. The paint in San Juan Red Ware is often polished into the surface of the pot. The decorations on Abajo Red-on-orange are poorly executed with wide wavy lines or wide straight lines in a variety of layouts (Plates 8, 9, and 10). The balance, or composition, of the layouts is generally good. Common design elements are concentric circles, rows of triangles, checkerboards, and terraced figures. Rims are usually rounded or flattened and unpainted. The temper is sand and rock fragments in varying proportions.

Throughout its range Abajo Red-on-orange was made from A.D. 700 to 850, but on Mesa Verde it was made during early Pueblo I times, circa A.D. 750 to 800. The range of this type is north of the San Juan River from the Animas River Valley west to the Colorado River. It is much more common in the western part of its range in southeastern Utah. The type site is Abajo 7:13 on Alkali Ridge, Utah, where this type is the most

common ware. It is probable that Abajo Red-on-orange was not made on Mesa Verde (Breternitz, 1982). It seems likely that it was brought in from the villages to the west.

The most common shapes in the Abajo Red-on-orange type are bowls, necked jars, seed jars, cups, and pitchers. Jar handles are formed of pierced lugs. Abajo Black-on-gray (Brew, 1946) is an overfired deviation of this type. A rare variation of Abajo Red-on-orange, known as Abajo Polychrome (Brew, 1946), has both reddish paint made of iron oxide and black paint of manganese or organic paint. Otherwise, this variety is identical to Abajo Red-on-orange. Abajo Polychrome has not been found on Mesa Verde.

Abajo Red-on-orange is distinguished from the later Bluff Black-on-red by its coarser and less well-executed designs that more commonly fill the field. The paint is redder and the surface more frequently orange than on Bluff Black-on-red (Plate 10).

Bluff Black-on-red was made from A.D. 750 to 900 (Morris, 1939; Roberts, 1930). It is usually unslipped and decorated with iron oxide or manganese pigments. The red iron paint is more common in the sites to the west of Mesa Verde. The most common forms of this type are bowls, jars, seed jars, and pitchers. Brick red is the predominant surface color, and the most common temper is crushed rock with some sherds having crushed potsherd temper. Designs are more carefully executed than in Abajo Red-on-orange. The designs are organized in a bilateral layout with one half reflecting the other. Much of the field is usually left unpainted. Designs of wide lines pendant from the rim are frequent. Rarely anthropomorphic or zoomorphic figures are present. Rims are usually flattened and sometimes painted (Figures 79 and 80).

The range of Bluff Black-on-red is the same as Abajo Red-on-orange, except that the former is found south of the San Juan River in the drainage of Chinle Wash. The type site for Bluff Black-on-red is NA2659 near

Bluff, Utah. Bluff Black-on-red has a blacker paint and usually a redder surface than Abajo Red-on-orange. Deadmans Black-on-red can be separated from Bluff Black-on-red by the presence of a slip in the former and the differences in design styles. As with Abajo Red-on-orange, Bluff Black-on-red is uncommon throughout Mesa Verde.

The final red ware type found on Mesa Verde is Deadmans Black-on-red, also known as La Plata Black-on-red (Martin, 1939; Roberts, 1930). It is a Pueblo I to II type made from A.D. 800 to 1000. It is distinguished from the other San Juan red wares by its bright red slip. Nearly all vessels of this type are polished over the decoration. The temper is crushed igneous rock, mostly andesite. The iron/manganese paint used to paint the decoration is reddish black. The symmetrical layouts are usually composed of narrow parallel lines with the angles filled in to form solid triangles (Plate 11). Although the design styles differ, the vessel forms of Deadmans Black-on-red are similar to those of Bluff Black-on-red; rims are flattened or rounded and are often solidly painted. The range of this type is the same

as that of Abajo Red-on-orange. The Mesa Verde type sites for Deadmans Black-on-red are Sites 1 and 102 on Chapin Mesa (O'Bryan, 1950).

The San Juan red wares on Mesa Verde were most common during the two centuries from A.D. 750 to 950. The fact that these types are restricted temporally makes them useful as horizon markers for their period of production. Compared to the white wares of the same period, all types of red ware are well made. The bowls, particularly Deadmans Black-on-red, are exceptionally symmetrical; they have thin, even walls, and the surfaces are well smoothed or polished. This is an indication that they may have been made elsewhere and came to Mesa Verde through some form of human interaction. It is not known whether any of the San Juan red ware types were made on Mesa Verde, but the present evidence indicates that these rare types originated in the Anasazi villages to the west in Utah (Breternitz, 1982). Red wares found on Mesa Verde sites dated after A.D. 1050 probably came from areas beyond the range of San Juan Red Ware, such as White Mountain Red Ware or Tsegi Orange Ware.

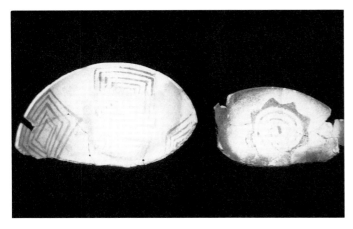

Fig. 79. Bluff Black-on-red bowl fragments with typical designs. Badger House Community, MVNP.

Fig. 80. Bluff Black-on-red bowl fragments with typical designs. Badger House Community, MVNP.

Intrusive Pottery

Many prehistoric sites on Mesa Verde contain a few sherds or an occasional restorable vessel of pottery types that were made beyond the northern San Juan area. The amount of intrusive pottery is insufficient to draw specific conclusions concerning prehistoric interaction, but they do give some indication of general temporal patterns of human interaction in the prehistoric Southwest.

In addition to the previously discussed San Juan Red Ware, which was probably produced to the west in southeastern Utah, the three intrusive wares most common on Mesa Verde are Cibola White Ware, White Mountain Red Ware, and Tsegi Orange Ware. Representative sherds of these wares are shown in Plate 12. In addition, a few earlier sherds of Lino Gray and Kana-a Gray have been identified. Traces of wares from the Mogollon Culture to the south and from the Fremont people to the west have also been recovered on Mesa Verde. The time periods of manufacture of the intrusive types are shown in Table 3.

Cibola White Ware is the predominant intrusive black-on-white pottery on Mesa Verde. The production of this ware was centered in the many sites of Chaco Wash and into the outliers, including some in the Mesa Verde area. The main time period of production of these types was A.D. 850 to 1150. The two most prevalent types of this ware found on Mesa Verde are Escavada Black-on-white (A.D. 925-1125) and Gallup Black-on-white (A.D. 1000-1150). Chaco Black-on-white (A.D. 1050-1200) is apparently less common on Mesa Verde, but it may be that this type is difficult to visually distinguish from Mancos Black-on-white, which has similar designs. Also present on Mesa Verde is Red Mesa Black-on-white (A.D. 875-950), an earlier Cibola White Ware type. It may be visually confused with Cortez Black-on-white, which has similar painted designs. Sherds of these three Cibola White Ware types are illustrated in the upper row of Plate 12. Traces of a fourth Cibola type known as Kiatuthlanna Black-on-white (A.D. 800-875) have also been recovered on Mesa Verde. The relative frequency of Cibola White Ware as compared to white wares from other areas indicates a greater interaction with the Chaco area during the period of A.D. 850 to 1150. This seems reasonable considering the Chaco influences on the outlying sites in the northern San Juan area around Mesa Verde.

Other than San Juan Red Ware, the most common intrusive red pottery on Mesa Verde is White Mountain Red Ware which was produced in sites in east-central Arizona and west-central New Mexico from A.D. 850 to 1250. Wingate Black-on-red (A.D. 850-950), with its distinctive, balanced, fine-hatched and solid designs, is easily identified in Mesa Verde sites. Puerco Black-on-white is less common, but it may be confused with Deadmans Black-on-red. Two later polychrome types of this ware are also found in small amounts on Mesa Verde. These are Wingate (synonyms: Houck or Querino) Polychrome (A.D. 1200-1250) and St. Johns Polychrome (A.D. 1100-1200). These White Mountain Red Ware types are widely dispersed in the Southwest, and Mesa Verde is near the northern limit of their occurrence. Sherds of these types from various sites on Mesa Verde are shown in rows 3 and 4 of Plate 12.

Tsegi Orange Ware is the third relatively common intrusive ware found on Mesa Verde. It was produced to the southwest in northeastern Arizona circa A.D. 1050 to 1300. Tusayan Black-on-red (A.D. 1050-1150) has heavy-hatched designs that are easily recognized among the other common types on Mesa Verde. Tusayan Polychrome has broad bands of red outlined in black on an orange background and was produced over a long period, from A.D. 1050 to 1300. Sherds of these two Tsegi Orange types from Mesa Verde are shown in row 4 of Plate 14.

Nearly all of the scarce restorable intrusive vessels found on Mesa Verde are White Mountain Red Ware.

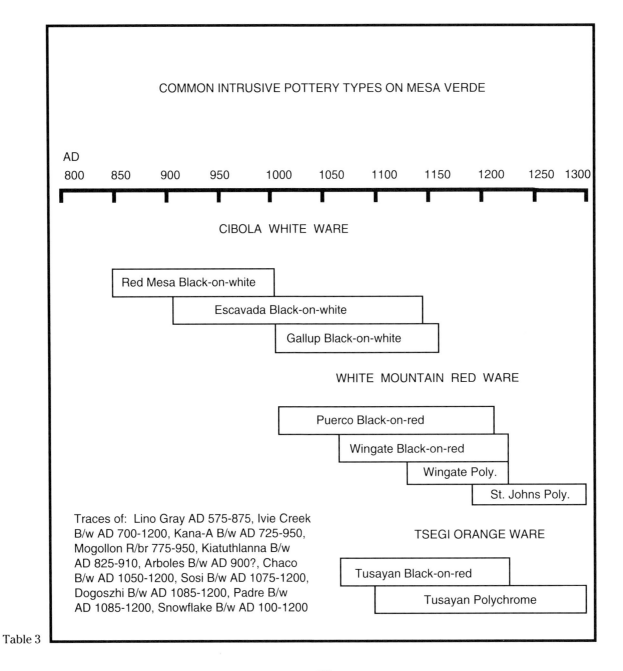

COMMON INTRUSIVE POTTERY TYPES ON MESA VERDE

AD
800   850   900   950   1000   1050   1100   1150   1200   1250 1300

CIBOLA WHITE WARE

Red Mesa Black-on-white

Escavada Black-on-white

Gallup Black-on-white

WHITE MOUNTAIN RED WARE

Puerco Black-on-red

Wingate Black-on-red

Wingate Poly.

St. Johns Poly.

Traces of: Lino Gray AD 575-875, Ivie Creek
B/w AD 700-1200, Kana-A B/w AD 725-950,
Mogollon R/br 775-950, Kiatuthlanna B/w
AD 825-910, Arboles B/w AD 900?, Chaco
B/w AD 1050-1200, Sosi B/w AD 1075-1200,
Dogoszhi B/w AD 1085-1200, Padre B/w
AD 1085-1200, Snowflake B/w AD 100-1200

TSEGI ORANGE WARE

Tusayan Black-on-red

Tusayan Polychrome

Table 3

Restorable St. Johns Polychrome bowls were found at Mug House and Spring House in the western part of the Park. In 1908, J.A. Jeancon found a beautiful whole Puerco Black-on-red pitcher in the trash slope below Step House. A Wingate Black-on-red pitcher was excavated at Site 34 in Little Soda Canyon during the Gila Pueblo excavations in 1950. Two other restorable intrusive vessels, a Tsegi Orange kiva jar and a possible Mogollon Red-on-brown bowl, were found at Site 34.

The intrusive pottery from Mesa Verde indicates that the most frequent interaction during Pueblo I to II was with the Chaco people to the south. We know that the prehistoric Chaco road system extended as far north as the San Juan River and may have extended into the Mesa Verde area. During Pueblo III the interaction seems to have been primarily with the White Mountain and Kayenta areas to the southwest. The presence of intrusive pottery does not necessarily imply contact between Mesa Verdeans and the pottery's producers because it may have been traded to one or more intermediate groups, or a few "professional" traveling traders may have made a living by trading goods throughout the region.

Mesa Verde White Ware Beyond Its Traditional Range

There have been a number of isolated finds of a few sherds or a single vessel of Mesa Verde White Ware in sites beyond its traditional range in the northern San Juan area. These are interpreted as evidence of interaction between the Mesa Verdeans and their neighbors.

Large amounts of pottery that is similar in style to Mesa Verde Black-on-white has been found at several post-abandonment (A.D. 1300) sites along the Rio Grande, indicating a possible migration of Mesa Verdeans to these areas. Although this pottery is made with local materials, some of the black-on-white pottery at these sites is very similar to Mesa Verde Black-on-white or McElmo Black-on-white.

Large concentrations of Mesa Verde-type black-on-white pottery were first reported in the Galisteo Valley south of Santa Fe, New Mexico. This valley contains several large adobe and masonry pueblos dating from A.D. 1300 to 1680. A carbon-painted pottery, similar to Mesa Verde Black-on-white, found at these sites has been named Galisteo Black-on-white (Kidder and Amsden, 1931). It is also called "Crackle Type" because the crackling of the thick white slip is similar to that on some Mesa Verde Black-on-white. The range of Galisteo Black-on-white extends east to Pecos Pueblo and south down the Rio Grande to the Albuquerque vicinity. The type site is Forked Lightning Ruin (LA672), near Pecos Pueblo. Galisteo Black-on-white has been included in Mesa Verde White Ware by Leland Abel (1955), but other researchers disagree with this assignment. It is dated from A.D. 1300 to 1400, which is soon after most of the northern San Juan region was abandoned.

Pottery found at the Gallinas Spring Pueblo (LA1178), farther south along the Rio Grande near Magdalena, New Mexico, is very similar to Mesa Verde Black-on-white. It has been named Magdalena Black-on-white (Knight and Gomolak, 1981). Helene Warren has pointed out how similar some of this pottery is to McElmo Black-on-white (1974). Gallinas Spring Pueblo is a five-hundred-room masonry pueblo occupied circa A.D. 1250 to 1325. Emma Lou Davis (1962, 1964), who has investigated possible migrations of the Mesa Verde people, believes this pottery, which she calls Mesa Verde Black-on-white, Magdalena Variety, is evidence of the migration of people from the Mesa Verde area south to the Gallinas Spring site.

Still farther south down the Rio Grande, more than 250 air miles from Mesa Verde, near Truth or Consequences, New Mexico, carbon-painted black-on-white pottery resembling Mesa Verde Black-on-white has been recovered. The site in this area is a cluster of large pueblos on Palomas Creek, northwest of Truth or

Consequences. This black-on-white type is not similar to any of the earlier local Mogollon types found in this area. In order to avoid the confusion of another new type name, Stephen Lekson has named this pottery *affinis* Magdalena Black-on-white (1986).

Whether the large amounts of Mesa Verde-like pottery in these three areas were produced by persons who migrated from the northern San Juan, or the designs and other similarities were transmitted to local potters, has been debated for some time. It is my belief that the evidence strongly supports the movement of people who were making Mesa Verde White Ware to these areas from some area to the north. The migration to these areas may have taken some time, so it

cannot be held that they should still be considered Mesa Verdeans, but wherever they came from they were still making pottery similar to the distinctive Pueblo III white ware of the northern San Juan area.

The vessel forms made in these types of Mesa Verde-like pottery are similar to those made in the original range, despite the appearance of some local forms. However, it is notable that Mesa Verde-style mugs and kiva jars were not made in the post-abandonment sites. One explanation for this is that these forms were used in religious ceremonies that were no longer performed after the Mesa Verdeans left their homeland (Bradley, p.c. 1989).

CONCLUSION

The development of pottery making in the Mesa Verde area in the late sixth century was probably the result of influence from the Anasazi or Mogollon peoples to the south. Pottery production continued because of its value to the increasingly sedentary population gathering in larger communities. Pottery forms, designs, and functions became traditional and were passed down form one generation to the next.

Tradition played an important role in the development of pottery in the Southwest (Peckham, 1990). The previous discussions of the manufacture, functions, and development of pottery on Mesa Verde over seven centuries indicate how persistent pottery traditions were and how slowly they changed. The lack of abrupt changes in pottery traditions indicates a lack of catastrophic changes or mass migrations into this area. Although there are historic examples of an individual's influence on pottery traditions (such as the revival of pottery similar to the older types by the Hopi/Tewa potter Nampeyo in the late nineteenth century), there is no evidence that single individuals brought about significant changes in prehistoric Mesa Verde pottery.

Pottery traditions are sometimes influenced by pottery from other areas. San Juan Red Ware was brought into Mesa Verde from southeastern Utah for about three hundred years, but produced little change in the local white and gray wares. Although they have not been carefully studied, the trade wares discussed in the last chapter also seem to have had little influence on the local pottery. One exception to this is that the designs on Red Mesa Black-on-white and Kiatuthlanna Black-on-white made in the Chaco area to the south may have influenced the makers of Cortez Black-on-white. Another possibility is that the overall designs with the hatched background on Mesa Verde Black-on-white were inspired by the designs on the intrusive Wingate Black-on-red and Wingate Polychrome from the White Mountain area of east-central Arizona.

The influence of tradition on Mesa Verde pottery forms and designs seems to have been stronger during Pueblo III times than in earlier periods. The forms and painted designs became more standardized and distinctive. The Mesa Verde mug and kiva jar forms were developed during this time and became characteristic of this period. The designs on Pueblo III Mesa Verde

Black-on-white became easily distinguishable from those on contemporary pottery made in other branches of the Anasazi.

Tradition helps to maintain order in a community, rewarding those who follow the traditional behaviors and punishing those who deviate. In historic Pueblo society, the welfare of the community and its individuals was believed to be dependent upon everyone behaving in accord with established norms. The increasing similarities in forms and designs during the later years of the Anasazi inhabitation of Mesa Verde may have resulted from the need to hold the community together during the drought and attendant disruptions during the final quarter of the thirteenth century.

Some pottery traditions cover a rather limited geographical area. Although it was distributed more widely, the production of San Juan Red Ware was limited to a relatively small area in southeastern Utah, from around the Abajo Mountains south to the vicinity of Bluff, Utah, on the San Juan River.

Although much remains unknown about the ceremonial use of pottery among the Mesa Verde Anasazi, a few tentative conclusions can be drawn based on the context of excavated vessels and the use of pottery in historic Pueblo ceremonial practices. Corn was the most important food source for the Mesa Verdeans. Today, corn meal and pollen play an important part in some Pueblo ceremonies, and this may have been the case in prehistoric times as well. Small jars or bowls used to hold the sacred corn meal or pollen would have acquired ceremonial importance. Kiva jars are more commonly found in kivas than in other rooms; this may indicate a possible ceremonial use. Some of these uncommon jars have four pairs of holes around the rim, which appear to have been used to secure the lids of the jars with twine. This type of vessel may have been used to store the precious selected seeds for planting the next spring or other small objects with ceremonial significance to the Anasazi.

The double mug is another very rare pottery form produced mainly during Pueblo III times. In examining over five hundred Mesa Verde-style mugs I found only six of the double-mug variety. If these had ceremonial use, it must have been in a very rarely held ceremony. Clay pipes are also scarce in the prehistoric sites on Mesa Verde. They are used today as "cloud blowers" in some Native American religious ceremonies. It would appear that in prehistoric times they were used only by religious leaders or were shared by participants in ceremonies. "Cigarettes" made of hollow reeds are also found in Mesa Verde sites, but the scarcity of all smoking implements suggests that smoking may have been a ceremonial practice rather than an everyday occurrence.

Pottery effigies of animals are rare and human effigies nearly nonexistent in the prehistoric sites of Mesa Verde. The significance of these materials is now lost.

One figure depicted on some Pueblo II and III bowls is known today by the Hopi name "Kokopelli." This figure, which appears to be a humpbacked man playing a flute, is found in many parts of the northern Southwest: in petroglyphs and pictographs on cliff walls, painted on walls of rooms, painted on pottery vessels, and carved into the stone floor of a kiva at Duckfoot Pueblo northwest of Cortez, Colorado. Kokopelli also appears as a kachina in some Hopi dances. Over the centuries the original significance of this figure has probably changed. Today, he is variously interpreted as a flute playing trader with a backpack, an insect with a long stinger, or a symbol of fertility.

Pueblo World View and Pottery

The traditional Pueblo people of today, and probably their Anasazi ancestors, have a more holistic view of the world than do most persons of European heritage. Consistent with the Pueblo view is the belief in the oneness of everything in the world. Traditional Pueblo people do not make the rigid distinction between living and nonliving things that is drawn by non-Indians. Everything in the world is seen as interrelated and having its own spirit. Pueblos see the earth as the mother of all things. Therefore, when mother earth (clay) is correctly combined with two other basic elements—water and fire—the resulting pottery is part of Mother Earth and has its own spirit.

Some Pueblo potters believe the spirit in the clay will influence the vessel form and the design painted on it. The potter makes some choices, but the final form and design are influenced by the clay. Some modern non-Indian potters who build hand-formed pots in the old manner also say the clay influences the form of their product. They say they cannot force the clay into a form against its will, implying a deterministic element in the clay.

Another important consideration in the making of Pueblo pottery is that it is made by women; this was probably the case in prehistoric times as well. Today there are a few male potters, but they are the exception. Women, being the mothers of all children, are closer to mother earth, and the pottery they make has a close affinity to the basic elements of the earth. As is the case today, it is probable that in prehistoric times the older women taught the girls and young women the potter's craft and that some families became noted for the skill of their potters.

Some Pueblo people believe that even the pieces of an old broken pot still have a spirit in them. As they walk across the sherd-covered villages of their ancestors they can hear the faint spirit songs on the wind. Perhaps, if you listen and believe, you too will hear such a song coming from the ancient vessels of the Anasazi.

GLOSSARY

Andesite. A dark-colored, volcanic rock that was crushed and used as temper in pottery and for ground stone tools such as mauls and axes.

Basketmaker III (A.D. 450 to 700). The stage during which the Mesa Verdeans developed pithouse villages, pottery, the bow and arrow, and the cultivation of corn, beans, and squash.

Bilateral symmetry. A concept of pottery design whereby the piece contains the same elements on opposing sides of a dividing line.

Burnish. A method of producing a polished surface on unfired pottery while the clay is leather-hard by rubbing it with a hard, smooth object. The rubbing compacts and aligns surface particles giving the vessel a high-gloss appearance.

Carbon paint (organic). Pigments that are derived from plants—often the Rocky Mountain beeweed or tansy mustard. When fired in a neutral or reducing atmosphere, the carbon pigment turns black.

Carbon streak. A black or gray zone in the interior cross section of a vessel wall, usually caused by incomplete removal of carbonaceous matter during low-temperature firing.

Carbonaceous shale. Shale containing carbon (organic matter).

Clay. One of several hydrous alumina-silicate minerals that are formed by decomposition of rock, chiefly granite, and have the property of plasticity.

Coil-and-scrape method. Hand-building a vessel by adding successive coils, or ropes, of clay, and smoothing and thinning the walls by scraping.

Crackling (crazing). A fine network of cracks on the surface of a vessel, caused by shrinking variation between the clay and slip.

Ethnography. The systematic recording of human cultures.

Fire cloud. A darkened area on a vessel's surface resulting from uneven firing and the deposit of carbon in the pores of the clay during firing.

Hohokam culture (300 B.C. to A.D. 1200). An agricultural culture in south-central Arizona, characterized by adaptation to desert and riverine environments.

Intrusive pottery. Pottery not locally produced, but brought in through trade or other forms of human interaction.

Iron-rich concretions (nodules). Nodular or irregular concentrations of iron, silica, lime, or other materials formed by localized deposition from solution in sedimentary rocks.

Kaolin. A soft, white nonplastic clay composed principally of the mineral kaolinite (a hydrated silicate of aluminum), commonly used in making ceramics.

Kiln. An enclosed, or partially enclosed, construction for firing ceramic materials.

Kiva, also kin kiva (a Hopi word). Generally a circular subterranean room, less than twenty feet in diameter and about seven feet high, with a roof hatchway for access. Especially during Pueblo III times and before, the kiva was associated with living quarters and was utilized by related family members for rituals, family gathering, and as a work area for weaving and production of other articles such as clothing and tools.

Kokopelli. The ubiquitous hump-backed fluteplayer; a symbol of fertility, depicted in rock art and pottery throughout the Anasazi area.

Leather-hard. Clay that is dried to a point at which the individual clay particles touch and the vessel body is rigid, but retains sufficient moisture to be carved or joined.

Lug handle. A short vessel handle that protrudes like an ear.

Mancos shale. The lowermost exposed formation on Mesa Verde, composed of soft marine shales and interbedded limestones; used by the Anasazi for pottery clay.

Mano. A rectangular-shaped stone moved back and forth on a metate to produce a grinding action.

Mesa Verde group. Three sedimentary formations overlying the Mancos shale; they are known as the Point Lookout, Menefee, and Cliff House formations.

Metate. A large stone on which the mano is moved to grind maize, seeds, clays, temper, or other substances.

Mineral paint. Paint made of finely ground iron or manganese mixed with water or an organic medium.

Mogollon culture (A.D. 300 to 1200). A prehistoric, horticultural people inhabiting western and central New Mexico and southeastern Arizona, typified by adaptation to mountain and transition ecological zones.

Montmorillonite. An important clay mineral; it is composed of hydrated silicate of calcium and/or magnesium and is the chief constituent of bentonite (a clay that swells readily when combined with moisture).

Neckbanded. A vessel that has visible flattened, but unsmoothed, coils around the neck.

Olla. A large, small-mouthed pottery jar used to transport and store water.

Open designs. Designs having a large proportion of the surface unpainted.

Organic medium. A carbon residue derived from plants which when mixed with a mineral pigment facilitates bonding of the paint to the surface of the vessel.

Out-turned rim. Also everted rim. A vessel rim that does not continue the line of the wall, but turns outward at an angle; characteristic of Mesa Verde Corrugated.

Oxidizing atmosphere. A firing condition characterized by an abundance of free oxygen, which combines with elements (such as iron) in the clay and yields clear colors on the surface of the vessel.

Paddle-and-anvil method. The process of thinning a vessel wall by holding an anvil of stone or other hard material on the interior of the wall and striking the exterior with a small flat paddle.

Plasticity. The property of a material that enables it to be shaped when wet and to hold this shape when the shaping force is removed.

Polychrome ware. Pottery having three or more surface colors.

Porosity. The volume of minute open spaces, or pores, in a solid, such as a ceramic object.

Reducing atmosphere. A condition of firing in which oxygen is removed from materials due to the presence of agents such as hydrogen or carbon.

Replication. A facsimile or reproduction of an original object.

Sherd, also potsherd. A term archaeologists use to refer to a broken fragment of pottery.

Sintering. A process of partially welding, or making a solid mass of, a particulate material by heating it close to the boiling point but not melting it.

Sipapu (from the Hopi word, *sipap*). A small, lined hole in the floor of a kiva or pithouse, possibly symbolic of the original emergence of the Anasazi ancestors from the underworld.

Spalling (lime popping). The flaking off of small pieces of the surface of a pottery vessel, often caused by the absorption of water by calcium carbonate or other substances.

Surface manipulations. The treatment of the plastic surface of a vessel by pinching, punching, incising, adding clay, or leaving the coils unsmoothed to produce a texture or design.

Temper. A material, mineral or organic, usually nonplastic, added to clay to improve its working, firing, or drying properties. Common examples of temper are crushed igneous rock, sand, or ground potsherds.

Terra cotta. An earthenware pottery, unglazed and usually red, relatively coarse and porous and low-fired (fired at less than 1000°C).

Thermal analysis. The refiring of sherds to determine their firing conditions and constituent materials.

Thermal shock resistance. The ability of a ceramic object to withstand sudden changes in temperature or repeated cycles of heating and cooling (thermal stress) without damage.

Tree-ring dating, also dendrochronology. A method of determining the age of timber through the pattern combination of annual growth rings of trees.

Truncated cone. Cone with the pointed end removed.

Type. A group of pottery vessels that are alike in every important characteristic, with the possible exception of shape.

Type site. The archaeological site from which the original type sherds were gathered. (Type sherds are preserved in a repository where they are available for later comparisons and study.)

Vitrification. The action or process of becoming glass; the high-temperature process whereby the particles within a mass fuse, closing the surface pores and forming a homogeneous, impervious mass without deformation.

Ware. A class of pottery whose members share similar technology, fabric, and surface treatment.

Wash. An impermanent coat of clay, usually containing iron, that is applied to the vessel after firing.

Water smoking. Removal of mechanically held water during the early stages of firing a pottery vessel.

BIBLIOGRAPHY

Abel, Leland J.
1955   San Juan Red Ware, Mesa Verde Gray Ware, Mesa Verde White Ware, and San Juan White Ware. Pottery types of the Southwest 5A, 10A, 10B, and 12A. *Museum of Northern Arizona Ceramic Series* 3B. Flagstaff, Arizona.

Blinman, Eric
1989   Potluck in the protokiva: ceramics and ceremonialism in Pueblo I villages. In *The Architecture of Social Integration in Prehistoric Pueblos.* Occasional Paper No. 1. William D. Lipe and Michelle Hegmon, eds. Crow Canyon Archaeological Center, Cortez, Colorado.

Bradley, Bruce
1989   Anasazi pottery making. In Margaret A. Heath, ed., *Teacher's Guide to Archaeological Activities.* Crow Canyon Archaeological Center, Cortez, Colorado.

Breternitz, David A.
1966   An appraisal of tree-ring dated pottery in the Southwest. *Anthropological Papers of the University of Arizona* 10. Tucson.
1982   The Four Corners Anasazi ceramic tradition. *The Arizona Archaeologist* 15:129-148. Arizona Archaeological Society, Phoenix.

Breternitz, David A., Arthur H. Rohn, and Elizabeth A. Morris
1984   Prehistoric ceramics of the Mesa Verde region, 2d ed. *Museum of Northern Arizona Ceramic Series* 5. Flagstaff. (Published by Interpark, Cortez, Colorado.)

Brew, John O.
1946   Archaeology of Alkali Ridge, southwestern Utah. *Papers of the Peabody Museum of American Archaeology and Ethnology* 21. Cambridge, Massachusetts.

Colton, Harold S.
1953   Potsherds: An introduction to the study of prehistoric southwestern ceramics and their use in historic reconstruction. *Museum of Northern Arizona Bulletin* 25. Flagstaff.

Davis, Emma Lou
1962   The Magdalena problem: A study which integrates a new pottery variety within the Mesa Verde design tradition. Manuscript on file at the Mesa Verde Museum, Mesa Verde National Park, Colorado.
1964   Anasazi mobility and Mesa Verde migrations. Doctoral dissertation. University of California, Los Angeles.

Fewkes, Jesse W.
1923   Archaeological field-work on the Mesa Verde National Park. *Smithsonian Miscellaneous Collections: Explorations and Field Work for 1922* 74(5):90-115. Washington.

Fuller, Steven L.
1984   Late Anasazi pottery kilns in the Yellow Jacket district, southwestern Colorado. *CASA Papers* 4. Cortez, Colorado.

Gratz, Kathleen
1976   The phallic handle attachment point: A problem in prehistoric ceremonialism. *Pottery Southwest* 3(4):7. Albuquerque.

Hayes, Alden C.
1964   The archaeological survey of Wetherill Mesa, Mesa Verde National Park. *National Park Service Archaeological Series* 7. Washington.

Kelley, J. Charles and Ellen Abbot Kelley
1975   An alternative hypothesis for the explanation of Anasazi culture history. In *Collected Papers in honor of Florence Hawley Ellis*, Theodore R. Frisbie, ed. *Papers of the Archaelogical Society of New Mexico* 2, Albuquerque.

Kidder, Alfred V. and Charles A. Amsden
1931   *The Pottery of Pecos, Vol. I.* Yale University Press, New Haven, Connecticut.

Knight, Terry L. and Andrew R. Gomolak
1981   *The Ceramics of LA1178, Gallinas Springs, New Mexico.* Cibola National Forest, Albuquerque.

Lekson, Stephen H.
1986   Mesa Verde-like ceramics near Truth or Consequences, New Mexico. *Pottery Southwest* 13(4):1-3. Albuquerque.

Martin, Paul S.
1936   Lowry Ruin in southwestern Colorado. *Field Museum of Natural History, Anthropology Series* 23(1). Chicago, Illinois.

Morris, Earl H.
1939   Archaeological studies in the La Plata district in southwestern Colorado and northwestern New Mexico. *Carnegie Institute of Washington Publication No. 519.* Washington.

Nordenskiold, Gustav E.A.
1893   *The Cliff Dwellers of Mesa Verde, Southwestern Colorado, Their Pottery and Implements.* P.A. Norstedt & Soner, Stockholm. (Reprints by The Rio Grande Press, 1979, and Mesa Verde Museum Association, 1990.)

O'Bryan, Deric
1950   Excavations in Mesa Verde National Park, 1947-1948. *Medallion Papers* 39. Gila Pueblo, Globe, Arizona.

Oppelt, Norman T.
1984   Worked potsherds of the Southwest: Their forms and distribution. *Pottery Southwest* 11(1): 1-6. Albuquerque.
1988   *Southwestern Pottery: An Annotated Bibliography and List of Types and Wares.* Scarecrow Press, Metuchen, New Jersey and London.
1989   The Mesa Verde style mug: Description of a distinctive prehistoric pottery form. *Southwestern Lore* 55(2):11-32. Boulder, Colorado.

Peckham, Stewart
1990   *From this Earth: The Ancient Art of Pueblo Pottery.* Museum of New Mexico Press, Albuquerque.

Rice, Prudence M.
1987   *Pottery Analysis: A Sourcebook.* University of Chicago Press, Chicago.

Roberts, Frank H.H.
1930   Early Pueblo ruins in the Piedra district, southwestern Colorado. *Bureau of American Ethnology Bulletin 96.* Smithsonian Institution, Washington, D.C.

Rohn, Arthur H.
1971   Mug House. Wetherill Mesa Excavation. *National Park Service Archeological Research Series* 7-D. Washington, D.C.
1977   *Cultural Change and Continuity on Chapin Mesa.* Regents Press, Lawrence, Kansas.

Rohn, Arthur H. and Jervis D. Swannack
1965   Mummy Lake Gray: a new pottery type. *Society for American Archaeology Memoir No. 19*, 14-18, Salt Lake City.

Schroeder, Albert H. (editor)
1982   Southwestern ceramics: A comparative review. *The Arizona Archaeologist* 15. Phoenix.

Shepard, Anna O.
1965   Ceramics for the archaeologist. *Carnegie Institute of Washington Publication No. 609.* Washington, D.C.

Swannack, Jervis D.
1969   Big Juniper House. Wetherill Mesa Excavations. *National Park Service Archaeological Research* 7-C. Washington, D.C.

Warren, A. Helene
1974   A southern variety of McElmo Black-on-white. *Pottery Southwest* 1(2):4. Albuquerque.

INDEX